Carson

CARSON

The Unauthorized Biography

Paul Corkery

Randt & Company

First Edition

Library of Congress Cataloging-in-Publication Data

Corkery, Paul, 1946—
    Carson : the unauthorized biography.

    Includes index.
    1. Carson, Johnny, 1925—   . 2. Television personalities—United States—Biography. I. Title.
PN1992.4.C28C67 1987   791.45'092'4 [B]   87-43083
ISBN 0-942101-00-6

Typesetting by Typographics, Ketchum, Idaho

Distributed to the trade by:
Kampmann & Company, Inc.
New York, NY

The author wishes to thank the following copyright holders for the privilege of quoting from their works: P.71—passage from the *New York Times*. Copyright ©1955, by the New York Times Company. Reprinted by permission. Pp. 92-95—passages from *P.S. Jack Paar*. Reprinted by permission of the William Morris Agency, Inc., on behalf of the Author. Copyright ©1983 by Jack Paar. Pp.104-106—passage from the *New York Times*. Copyright ©1962, by the New York Times Company. Reprinted by permission. Pp.106-107—passage from Bob Williams' column "On the Air." Reprinted by permission of the New York Post, copyright ©1962. Pp.138-143—passages from *Jack Benny: An Intimate Biography*. Reprinted by permission of The Putnam Publishing Group from *Jack Benny: An Intimate Biography* by Irving A. Fein. Copyright ©1976 by Irving A. Fein. P.170—passage from the *New York Times*. Copyright ©1980, by the New York Times Company. Reprinted by permission. P.189—passage from Liz Smith's column. Copyright ©1983 New York News, Inc. Reprinted with permission.

Printed in the United States of America

10 9 8 7 6 5 4 3 2 1

To Fred Allen

Acknowledgements

Eleanor Hoover, a reporter of extraordinary skill, diligence, sympathy, and insight, conducted for me the interviews in this book with the three former Mrs. Johnny Carsons: Ms. Jody Carson, Ms. Joanne Carson, and Ms. Joanna Carson. To Eleanor Hoover and these ladies, my thanks for their cooperation and their contributions. Many other current and former friends and co-workers of Johnny Carson also offered their insights, opinions, and memories. Some of these interviews were conducted by another fine reporter, Barbara Manning. To all, I owe thanks.

Across the country I have been aided by the work and memories of other journalists, whose pieces are cited within. I am very grateful to all, and am especially grateful to Ann Sausedo, the library director of the *Los Angeles Herald*, and also to Susan Vaughn, Rip Rense, Philip V. Brennan, Jr., Sy Presten, and Loreen Arbus. I wish also to thank those NBC staff members in New York and Los Angeles who went out of the way to be helpful. To Drue Wilson, Johnny Carson's secretary, my thanks for adept, courteous responses to my occasional queries. Likewise, the staffs at the New York Public Library, the Beverly Hills Public Library, the UCLA Library, and the Academy of Motion Picture Arts and Sciences were always helpful and cheerful.

In Los Angeles, two longtime students of that city's social life and the entertainment industry—Mrs. Mollie M. Sheklow and Gene Stoddard—were, as always, generous with their help and good wishes.

To Thomas D. Corkery of San Francisco, a special thanks for

his remarkable memory for Carson jokes and his generous, constant help.

To Dana Randt and Virginia Randt of Randt & Company, my particular thanks for suggesting that in the life of a performer I like there might be a book. I deeply appreciate as well their availing interest, Dana Randt's discerning eye and business acumen and, of course, Virginia Randt's proficient and salutary editing.

Finally, to Martha and Alarm, thanks for the talks, the walks, and the miles of Smilgis smiles.

Contents

Acknowledgements

1 Here's Johnny! 13

2 Pie Plates on the Roof 39

3 Carson's Cellar 53

4 Guest Shots, Best Shots,
   A Marriage Falls Apart 75

5 *The Tonight Show*'s Early Evenings 87

6 A Paar of New Shoes 97

7 From Employee to Midnight Idol 109

8 Tiny Tim and the Competition 125

9 'This Guy Can Kill You.' 133

10 'I Want to Meet Her.' 145

11 The Blockbuster Announcement 153

12 Bombastic Bushkin 163

13 Killer Labels 173

14 'What I'll Miss the Most . . .' 181

15 Joanna Speaks 199

16 In the Groove 211

17 The New Mrs. Carson 217

18 Shining Hour 227

   Index 235

Carson

1
Here's Johnny!...

He is grouchy in the mornings at Malibu when he awakes; indeed "grump hour" is what his new wife calls those first moments at Johnny Carson's home. To himself, as well as to many others, this seems odd. After all, when Johnny Carson awakes each morning, he not only awakes on one of the most stunning beach fronts in North America, he is also about $50,000 richer than he was when he went to bed. And he doesn't have to be at the job by nine.

Furthermore, he is a comedian, the national comedian. The grump who wakes up in Malibu is the winsome guy who sent America to sleep smiling, if not laughing. And while he's waking up, his jokes are being repeated in coffee shops, offices, factories, and schools across America. "Nonetheless," he has said, "I wake up rough."

So it's part of the daily routine that his small household—his wife Alexandra (or Alexis, as she is also known) Mass, a housekeeper, and a few other household helpers—give him a clear berth in the morning. He's never actually ugly, or mean; just unsociable, until he's had a chance to look at the ocean, watch some birds (the ornithological type) and some stars (the astronomical kind) still glimmering in the post-dawn light.

His rough risings trouble him, and he has apologized for them, though they are a common trait among comedians and humorists, including those Carson has admired and studied: Mark Twain's wife, Livy, was so appalled by Twain's gutter mood and language in the mornings that, one day, she copied down all the vile words he uttered. In the afternoon, she repeated them deadpan to Twain. The startled humorist looked at her and smiled and said, "Livy, you've got the words right, you just don't have the right tune." But Twain, like Carson, in deference to his beloved family, sought to take himself apart from the household until his askant morning mood had passed.

Fred Allen, the great radio topical comedian to whom Carson pays friendly homage every time a segment of the Mighty Carson Art Players appears, used his mornings to draw up sketches for the Mighty Allen Art Players that were often so vinegary they were never broadcast.

Groucho Marx, another man to whom morning became choleric, had, however, no hestitation about venting his peevishness on family, friends, and help. In his case, the household learned to avoid him, and his tongue.

Dawn, whether at 4:00 a.m. or at 2:00 p.m., is not an easy time for comics. There is no audience, and the raspy, angry sentiments which ultimately lie behind their humor seem then to be at their rawest.

And Johnny has the problem too, though he has the good grace to leave everyone alone until those first thoughts and feelings have begun to sort themselves into categories—categories acceptable for humor. Because once he's awake, and whether he's working that day or not, his first thoughts go into the making of the thing he's most famous for: *The Tonight Show* monologue. Only when that's under way, can his staff at Malibu start to brew the coffee. For Johnny—no matter how rich nor how secure— the job, the monologue, the show come first and foremost. It couldn't be any other way.

And on the morning we have in mind, a day shortly before Christmas 1986, the routine is the same. He is scheduled to tape another performance of *The Tonight Show* this afternoon. This will be about the five thousandth time he has appeared on *The Tonight Show* since he started hosting it twenty-five years ago on October 1, 1962. On this show, he will follow the format he has built over the years. He'll do a monologue followed by a skit or banter with Ed McMahon (called in *Tonight Show* parlance the "five-spot" because it's the fifth event on the show's schedule), he'll talk with two guests, and introduce a musical number and a magic act.

In Malibu, as Carson is still sipping his morning coffee, he begins to read the newspapers and make notes for his monologue. (An item about the layoff of AT&T workers has caught his eye.) At Carson's office in Burbank a team of writers is already preparing additional material that Carson might use that night. And outside Studio One, a number of the five hundred people who will make up the studio audience are already beginning to line up for tickets.

15

The Tonight Show Starring Johnny Carson—the official name, used even when a guest host is filling in—is the largest single moneymaker for the National Broadcasting Company. It has brought in advertising revenues of more than $50 million a year to the network, and has accounted for as much as 17 percent of the network's pre-tax profits.

Despite challenges over the years from other talk shows, late-night movies, and late-night news programs, *The Tonight Show*, which is regularly seen by between five million and nine million people, has been the top-rated late-night show on network television for as long as Carson has been hosting it.

Broadcast at 11:30 p.m. on the East and West coasts, its most enthusiastic and loyal audiences see it at 10:30 p.m. These are the audiences in the midwestern, mountain, and plains states. Television's rating specialist, A. C. Nielsen Company, reports that in a belt of thirteen states stretching from Illinois west to Idaho and from the Dakotas and Minnesota south through Missouri, Kansas, and Colorado, *The Tonight Show*'s popularity is unassailable.

To say *The Tonight Show* is "programmed" to the tastes of people in "the heartland" (as the TV executives, who seem almost frightened of these viewers, call this region) is to denigrate the genius of the show. It does not condescend to its viewers or pander to what it supposes their prejudices or proclivities might be. *The Tonight Show*, produced in Hollywood and hosted by one of the nation's richest men, is in fact created from the values and wit of the most stable, hard-working, and discerning part of the American nation—the American middle class, still the driving, if most beleagured, force in the nation.

The *Tonight Show* monologue focusses what middle-class America thinks about national events. Journalists quote it as evidence of the mood of the country; politicians dread it; and those far removed from the middle class scrutinize it. All of which is remarkable, since the man who utters the jokes doesn't live in the Midwest, nor is he a member of the middle class. Yet his sensibilities, beliefs, and values are still there.

For the last thirty-six years, Johnny Carson has lived in the most expensive and rarified parts of Los Angeles or New York, but his jokes and quips uncannily reflect the talk not of, say, the snootiest drawing rooms of Park Avenue, nor of the most barricaded baronetcies of pecking-order obsessed Beverly Hills, nor of the trendier-than-thou lofts of SoHo, nor the offices of bewildered Washington politicians and pundits, but rather of the morning coffee conversation of places like the Villa Inn Coffee Shop in Norfolk, Nebraska. Yet in all those other places—Park Avenue, Beverly Hills, and Capitol Hill—you will hear Johnny Carson's jokes repeated and laughed over. He is midwestern, but he is also hip, and exceedingly current and well informed.

That he is well informed is surprising because, by virtue of being a TV star, he is, and must be, insulated from the public. Ironically, television, which exposes the star to everyone, requires that the star be, for sanity's sake, insulated from the public. Or at least from that maddening and massive bottom-of-the-gene-pool part of the public that stupidly and weirdly is drawn to, and throws itself at, TV stars.

And the fans aren't the only pesky ones.

One of the banes of a TV star's existence is the rest of the entertainment industry which is populated by unlikeable types. "Everybody's after Johnny for a favor," says one TV old-timer who has watched the business grow up. "Every agent and public relations guy wants him to give a client a spot, and every starlet wants to be on the show. An appearance on *The Tonight Show* can make a career, and they'll make enormous pests out of themselves to get that shot. And many of these guys are pests to begin with."

So it's almost impossible, if you're a TV star, to get any input into your life about what's going on in the rest of the country. Hidden behind favor seekers and flatterers, a TV star is virtually isolated from real life.

But Johnny Carson does keep in touch. And the great triumph of his career may be that he has been able to stay in touch with the rest of the country and with the values of his childhood, despite a position, an income, and a style of living that requires the kind of insulation that often results in debilitating isolation. Maintaining contact has been hard work and has led to agonizing personal choices over the years, notably in his marriages. But remaining at the center of American life is his stock in trade, and he works at it each day.

That's why those grumpy first moments in the morning are important. He may apologize for them, but it's in those few minutes that Johnny manages to catch up with himself, to wash away the show business and Hollywood of the night before, and to muse on what America is thinking, reading, and seeing.

Johnny's part of the Malibu beach is perfect for the kind of solitary morning with the papers, coffee, cigarettes, and telephone that he likes. His home is far from the busy Malibu Colony further south, which is the usual haunt of celebrities. Johnny had once lived near the Colony, but he purchased his current Malibu home in 1985 for $8,650,000.

Formerly the home of Dorn Schmidt, a real estate developer who reportedly made a fortune harvesting and exporting macadamia nuts in Hawaii, it is an award-winning house built by the architect Ed Niles.

Positioned on a promontory that provides a spectacular view of Santa Monica Bay and surrounded by a huge buff-colored stucco wall, the well-guarded house looks like a villa one would find in Acapulco or on the Mediterranean. Covered with a glass roof, the home contains twelve thousand square feet of living space.

Architect Niles describes the home as "a large greenhouse set on a bluff . . . a huge glass roof with a forest inside." Outside Johnny is now building a sports complex, including tennis courts, which a neighbor describes as being "the size of a small duchy in France." The entire estate is guarded.

Johnny's art collection is extensive. "His taste in art is superb," says decorator Stuart Lampert, who with his partner, Steven Tomar, has worked on Carson's homes for eleven years. "He likes all kinds, by the way, but favors what is called 'contemporary.' Alexis Mass tends to like more traditional or realistic art."

The Carson collection includes paintings by David Hockney, Chuck Arnoldi, Guy Dill, and Paul Kane. He also has works by super-realist Alberto Man who paints only on men's clothing. The sculpture includes pieces by Robert Graham, Eugene Jardin, Peter Shire Mizumo, Betty Gold, Vasa, and James Havard.

This house replaces one which had become his permanent residence after he and Joanna, his third wife, separated in 1983. It was on the beach in front of that house that he met his fourth wife, Alexandra Mass, sometime after his separation. He later sold it to Tatum and John McEnroe.

After his divorce was finalized in 1985, he decided to buy a newer Malibu home. When he saw his current home, he had already made a down payment on another house. But after seeing what is now his spectacular retreat (curiously enough pointed out to him by the man who owned the house on which Johnny had already made the down payment), he cancelled the other deal.

Bob Newhart, upon entering the new home, said, "Where's the gift shop?" Billy Wilder (the acerbic director of such hits as *Some Like It Hot, The Apartment,* and *One, Two, Three*), who is a close friend of Carson and who has become something of an influence on Johnny, said more tellingly when he saw the living room of the new house, "Where's the desk?"

The living room does, in fact, look like a more spacious and posh version of the famous *Tonight Show* set. The show is never far from Carson.

The next step in the morning, after grump hour, the papers, coffee, and smiles, is the start of a day-long ritual known as "the calls." *Tonight Show* Executive Producer Fred de Cordova has been at his desk in the *Tonight Show* Burbank offices since about nine, and he will hear from Johnny several times that morning. Indeed, he hears from Johnny several times every day, whether or not Carson is actually going to be the host that night and whether or not Johnny is in Malibu, a New York apartment, London, or the south of France.

Once when being visited by *Los Angeles Times* reporter Paul Rosenfield, de Cordova stopped speaking in mid-sentence a few seconds before ten o'clock. At the exact stroke of the hour, de Cordova's phone line rang. "That'll be the ten o'clock call," de Cordova explained, and picked up the phone. After saying hello to Carson, de Cordova began his report. He remarked about the previous night's show, discussed a few additional ideas for the upcoming night's program, and engaged in a little intelligence talk. "There are travel warnings," de Cordova said cryptically into the phone. "There are various places it's better to stay out of. Now about tonight. You have Bette Davis, though you may have to lead her up the steps. Paul Provenza is on. Pete Fountain's on, doing clarinet numbers. Doc has that spot covered."

Then he hung up and resumed his interview with Rosenfield.

"The first call," explained another old *Tonight Show* hand, "is like the report of the dawn patrol. De Cordova fills Johnny in on the latest overnight doings in the jungle—that's the executive corridor at NBC—and with the general Hollywood gossip that Johnny ought to know. And Carson gives Fred any first-thing-in-the-morning thoughts he has on the upcoming show or shows, like ideas for sketches he wants the writers to get to work on, or guests he'd like to have on, or problems. The Joan Rivers blow-up—when Joan suddenly announced she was signing with the Fox Network—was a lead item on the ten o'clock call." From ten until Carson gets to work later in the day, around one or two, the calls continue.

Carson on vacation is continually briefed on what guests are planned for the substitute host and, more importantly, how the guest host is doing with the ratings, laugh-wise, and backstage. *The Tonight Show* is Johnny's, and no aspect of its operation is far from his attention.

But at home he does not sit, blithy or Bligh-like, by his phone rapping out orders and receiving information. The mornings after the grump hour and the dawn patrol intelligence report become considerably more human.

After breakfast, he's off to his old beach house for his almost daily tennis game (The tennis courts under construction at his new home are not yet finished). Avid about the game, he frequently plays in celebrity tournaments as well. His game is described by one expert "as pretty good but he's not a professional." Partners in Malibu often include Steve Lawrence and Charlton Heston.

After the game, there's sometimes a light lunch and a further perusal of the morning papers. He reads *USA Today,* the *Los Angeles Herald,* the *Los Angeles Times,* the *Wall Street Journal,* the *New York Times,* and the two local entertainment newspapers, *Variety* and the *Hollywood Reporter.*

Though the business lunch is a major institution of the entertainment industry (Some show-business execs, after years of consuming the ritual poached salmon at business lunches, have been known to drive their cars against the traffic on the freeway), Johnny Carson rarely, if ever, bothers with one. The activitity, he feels, spoils or vitiates the energy he wants to devote to the show. So no formal lunches when he might be expected to amuse or entertain, or even chat very much. Johnny's regimen gears his entire day to making the one hour he's on the air the best and freshest it can be. Why waste energy, humor, and wit early in the day? Especially on people who are looking for ways in which to use your fame, wit, and power?

In the early afternoon he sets off for the studio. While Malibu is full of actors and performers who make the thirty-six-mile commute along the Pacific Coast Highway, the Santa Monica Freeway, the San Diego Freeway, and the Ventura Freeway to the complex of studios in Burbank, Carson is one of the few who drives it by himself. He is rarely chauffeured. If any experience can help keep him in touch with the feelings and frustrations of the average man, it's that long, frustrating drive along the freeways, which even at one in the afternoon are rush-hour busy, as Los Angeles grows and grows.

The famous Delorean he once drove is gone, taken back by the Delorean creditors. (Only on loan to Carson for promotional purposes, the car was sold for $18,000 at auction in 1984 to a driver for an oil tool company.) Nowadays Carson usually drives his white Corvette, though he occasionally uses other cars he owns, including a Mercedes and a restored 1939 Chrysler, which his father had owned back in Norfolk, Nebraska.

It is in the Corvette that he makes his way to work today, recovered from the grump hour, relaxed by tennis, and buoyed by the knowledge, gleaned from the morning papers, that the madness of politicians, power companies, and Hollywood has not suddenly perished from the earth, leaving him without the material for a monologue.

The Tonight Show offices are located in the NBC acreage on Alameda Avenue in Burbank, a part of Los Angeles packed with movie and television studios, including those of Walt Disney, Warner Brothers, Columbia Pictures, and Universal Studios.

After Carson drives through a guarded gate, he follows a maze of driveways covered with speed bumps. Carson claims one of the bumps has been named in his honor by NBC. (Movie studios traditionally honor top stars by naming studios, commissaries, theaters, and sandwiches after their top moneymakers. The networks, who like to remind their stars of their ultimate power to cancel a program instantly, do nothing of the kind.)

The Tonight Show offices, which house a staff of about twenty-five, are in prefab buildings that the network chooses to call "bungalows," as if they were recreating the palmy era when movie stars were provided with real bungalows in which to lounge near the barn-like stages where they were filming. For the show that is NBC's most profitable, the office architecture is surprisingly modest, the buildings not so much bungalows as house trailers.

These trailer offices are not where *The Tonight Show* is taped. The studio where taping takes place is called Studio One, a typically barn-like area with a grandstand, one hundred feet away in the main complex.

CARSON

Outside the front door of the office is a parking area where Ed McMahon, Fred de Cordova, and Doc Severinsen all have spaces. Johnny parks his car around the corner in a studio street called "The Midway" where his space is marked by a sign, not a stencil on a curbstone. The locale was chosen to keep him from the glare of tourists' eyes, and the sign, which is guarded against theft, is the mark of a truly important person at NBC. Curbstone stencils are for lesser stars. The Midway is also the parking place for other top NBC personalities including Vanna White, Pat Sajak, and Dick Carson, Johnny's brother, who is not a star but is a game-show director.

Though the offices look from the outside as if they were designed to be naval supply depots-cum-officers' clubs in the Aluetians, inside the situation is cheerier. The colors and lighting are subdued, and tend towards earth tones, a favorite color choice with Carson, who has spent years surrounded by the garish metallic colors and intense lights of television stage sets. The light in the offices comes primarily from shaded electric lamps. Entering and being in *The Tonight Show* offices is a little like riding around in one of those lampshaded busses the Hertz people use to pick you up at the airport.

All of *The Tonight Show* execs and regulars—Severinsen, McMahon, de Cordova—have small private offices here. Johnny's is near the studio, nestled amid the back-stage rigging. De Cordova drives back and forth from Johnny's office in a golf cart.

On his coffee table are a set of drum sticks, long yellow legal pads, and the day's newspapers. Carson, remarkably, is one of the few TV performers who actually reads newspapers and magazines. That other talk-show hosts, and even news anchors, don't read papers and don't follow the news may sound incredible. But you have only to tune to a talk show or a news show to realize how uninformed and ignorant most TV people are. In some cases, it's sheer vanity on the part of performers to think that they can go before the public and not know anything of the world they jointly inhabit. But in most cases, TV performers don't keep up with the news because they don't think it's important and they are simply too busy.

That someone who is on the air only an hour a day should be too busy to read the news is another statement that would seem to strain credulity, but it's true. TV is exhausting, time-consuming work, and just keeping up with the madness of the day in the studio is enough to deflect anyone's interest from the papers and the news. Of course, an ignorant talk-show host is an uninteresting one—forced to fall back on his old shtick for laughs—but few seem bothered by this.

It's a signal achievement for Carson that he does not allow his day to be eaten up with the technical aspects of TV work, and that he spends much of his time dealing with news, newspapers, and magazines.

At one time, he not only devoured newspapers and magazines, he also appeared in them regularly. Near his desk is a wall with framed magazine covers and stories about Carson that have appeared over the years, including Timothy White's extensive and fascinating *Rolling Stone* interview with him in 1979. There are also "still" photographs from the more recent interviews he's given, which have been on television, with Mike Wallace of *60 Minutes* and Barbara Walters on ABC. The magazine covers are from the sixties and early seventies—lately, printed journalism has lost its appeal for Carson. He has his public relations people routinely turn down all requests for interviews from magazine or newspaper reporters, even those offering him the unheard-of opportunity to edit and approve the story before it goes to press.

Carson's long-time secretary, the affable and efficient Drue Wilson, has a small office in the bungalow, where she functions as one of the best-liked and most powerful women in Hollywood, fending off intruders and greeting the elect. Also situated in the bunker are the offices for the writers and a group of people called the "talent coordinators."

Although Johnny's monologue is his own and its content unknown to anyone, including the writers, Ed McMahon, Fred de Cordova, and NBC—they hear it for the first time along with the audience—much of it is drafted for Johnny by a group of his writers. The rest of his staff of writers work on sketches and skits for segments like the Mighty Carson Art Players; Karnak the Magnificent; Art Fern's Tea Time Movie; and Floyd R. Turbo, American.

A few of Carson's writers, like Raymond Spiller and Kevin Mulholland, have been with him for years. Others last for only thirteen weeks, which is the union contract of minimum length. ("Welcome to Murder, Incorporated," Carson once said to a new employee on his first day of work.) Hollywood, nevertheless, is full of gag writers and jokesmiths eager for a chance to try out for work on *The Tonight Show,* where top writers earn well over $100,000 a year. The process by which they are chosen for thirteen-week tryouts is varied, but mostly it has to do with word of mouth in the Los Angeles community of joke writers. For years one of the most reliable sources of new writers was Joan Rivers.

Joan was famous for buying jokes from freelancers for virtually nothing. (Ten dollars a joke was the fee, according to one former Rivers writer who went on to work for *The Tonight Show.*) But she would recommend good writers to *The Tonight Show* for employment.

The monologue writers working for Carson produce jokes and

lines each day that Carson then reviews. Often the writers work on their own ideas, but they also develop themes that Carson suggests. "The monologue is my own," Johnny has said, "but no one could write an entire six- or seven-minute monologue each night all by himself. That's where the writers come in. They're absolutely essential. But I edit myself."

For years one writer had a sign over his desk which read "It was funny when it left here," but any implication that Johnny barks angrily at writers who produce bombs is incorrect. Johnny's writers over the years have reported that he, unlike most famous comics, rarely blames, and never berates, his writers for jokes that went wrong. As any viewer of the show knows from watching sequences at the desk when Johnny is going over material, he edits as he goes, and if he chooses a joke and it doesn't work, Johnny takes the blame.

This doesn't mean, however, that once you land a tryout as a writer on the show, it's easy to make the grade. Johnny has to choose your jokes, and choose a lot of them on a daily basis, for you to get the job.

A job—a regular job—on the Carson show is almost a guarantee of later success in comedy in Hollywood—not so much as a stand-up comic (though Dick Cavett had been a Carson writer) but as a writer or a producer on the situation comedies that Hollywood produces. David Lloyd and Ed Weinberger are two former Carson writers who have achieved enormous success as writers and producers of situation comedies. For years *The Mary Tyler Moore Show* and other shows produced by her company were staffed by former Carson writers like Lloyd and Weinberger. Lloyd is now one of the highest-paid writers in the world, much sought after by producers of television comedies. And Weinberger is now the head of Johnny's subsidiary production company, and has been responsible for its current revitalization with hits like the new show, *Amen,* starring Sherman (*The Jeffersons*) Helmsley. For a writer, a gig on the Carson show is what a degree from Harvard Business School is to an aspiring corporate type.

Carson meets with the writers on a regular, but hardly routine, schedule. Sometimes weeks can go by without a meeting with the writers—in those interim periods, any communication from the chief is handled by de Cordova. When Johnny does meet with writers, it's usually for a tone-setting session.

The production of comedy on a regular basis is tough, and the penalty for failure is a swift, severe, and painful silence. But not all jokes, of course, can get laughs.

Surprisingly, some jokes bomb because of the nuances of performing in a television studio. For instance, the third or fourth joke of the monologue usually produces no laughter at all. Even a very good joke wouldn't get laughter at that point, because it is just then that the people in the studio audience, keyed up and enthusiastic at the prospect of seeing Carson in person, are sitting back and simply looking at him, not listening. It takes a bad joke and a supposedly shocked Carson to bring them back to their senses again.

And bad jokes aren't always so terrible because Johnny likes to "save" or come out of them with a laugh. This dates back to Johnny's days as a teen-aged magician when he discovered that a trick that didn't work, when handled with the right kind of impish humor, could be as big a hit with an audience as one that did work. "My magic turned into comedy," Carson once said. Today part of his comedy *is* the magic to turn a bad joke into a laugh.

In the early afternoon, when Carson receives the manuscripts with the day's catch of jokes, he also receives an update from the talent coordinators, those staffers (about five) responsible for obtaining ("booking") the on-air "talent." (Talent is a show-business term that is used to describe anyone, performer or not, who appears on the air, whether actually talented or not.)

Some *Tonight Show* talent coordinators specialize in finding eccentric or interesting "civilians," as they are called in show business. Civilians are quite simply people who don't work in the entertainment industry and who, indeed, are not entertainers. *The Tonight Show* talent coordinators are charged with finding such folk to be guests on the show. But the talent coordinators don't always handle this task alone. A man in Malibu who had hired a carver to create a totem pole for the front of his store recalls one day when a flashy white sports car pulled off the road and parked near the pole that was being carved. The driver sat watching for a while and then came hustling out to talk to the carver. The driver was Johnny Carson, who was fascinated by the carver and his craft. A few weeks later, the carver was in the guest's seat on *The Tonight Show.*

A few of the talent coordinators, however, do nothing but deal with and fend off the hordes of Hollywood agents, publicists, managers, and would-be stars eager to get their clients or themselves on the air.

Exposure on *The Tonight Show* can turn an unknown into a contender, but surprisingly few Hollywood actors and actresses, no matter how accomplished on the studio stage, have what it takes to carry on a simple conversation, let alone a witty one. The late Rock Hudson knew his limitations and, in an interesting twist, forbade his manager from booking him on *The Tonight Show* since he felt he was incapable of carrying on an interesting conversation without a script. "I can't order from a menu without two writers working up my lines, " he once said in explanation. Others, particularly television stars, are not so shrewd, and Johnny has a real distaste for people who cannot really talk, except to plug their careers. Actors and actresses are usually all ego and little thought and thus have nothing to say that would interest anyone but themselves. That doesn't keep them from trying to get on the show, and *Tonight Show* talent coordinators, usually culled from the ranks of publicists and agents themselves, spend hours on the phone putting off hopefuls who would, however, be hopeless as guests.

This makes many enemies and has caused rumors about a *Tonight Show* blacklist. There really is no such list, though spurned agents often explain their failure (and sometimes boost their clients' egos) by telling them they are banned because Johnny doesn't like them. But no such blacklist exists. The ability to be an entertaining guest is what the coordinators care about.

The surprising but sad fact is that most actors often aren't entertaining, just persistent. That's how they got their jobs on their not-very-entertaining TV series in the first place. But determination alone does not result in a guest spot with Carson, though it does help if you're talented to begin with. Joan Rivers was turned down six times by *Tonight Show* talent coordinators before Carson, who had been hearing about her from friends who travel the nightclub circuit, gave her her first shot.

Talent coordinators also watch for people who perform unusual stunts, but less frequently now than in the past. Once a staple of *The Tonight Show*, the stunt act often featured derring-do, like fire eating or rope-ladder climbing. These acts—which usually included a segment in which Johnny, ever the good sport, tried to participate—resulted in pratfalls, near falls, and a surprisingly large number of successes. In the very early days of the show

Johnny went to Yankee Stadium to pitch to Mickey Mantle and Roger Maris; went to the desert to fly jets; and he performed other exotic stunts, such as tossing axes and actors around the set. Showing Johnny as a good sport, a kind of George Plimpton of middle America, was one of *The Tonight Show's* earliest missions. From time to time these stunts recur, but not as often as before. Even Mantle had to retire.

Talent coordinators also try to book guests and acts which will get *The Tonight Show* talked about in the nation's newspapers and magazines. The bizarre on-camera wedding of falsetto singer Tiny Tim and Miss Vicki in 1969 was perhaps the most notorious of these; it provoked enormous viewership and hundreds of articles and columns, many outraged.

Just as a few of *The Tonight Show's* writers have been around since the early days, so too have a number of the talent coordinators. Regular viewers are familiar with Johnny's frequent mentions of a staffer he calls "Crazy Shirley," who is, in fact, one Shirley Wood, the most senior of the show's talent coordinators. With Johnny since the early sixties, she, along with Ed McMahon and former writer Pat McCormick (who still occasionally phones in gags), were the three wild ones of *The Tonight Show,* famous for antic behavior and after-hours shenanigans.

Today life is calmer, and in the vastness of Los Angeles, *The Tonight Show* staff doesn't socialize as much as it did in the old days in New York, where the studio was surrounded by friendly bars and tolerant restaurants. The tone is more businesslike around *The Tonight Show* bungalows, and the staff is younger and more ambitious about "making it" in network television than in the past. But the emphasis remains on keeping the show fun.

In midafternoon, Carson attends to his own drafts of the

monologue and receives, via Fred de Cordova, any late word from the talent coordinators about the upcoming guests, most of whom were scheduled weeks earlier. Then, while musical rehearsals begin in Studio One, Carson deals with personal business and correspondence. Afterward, if there's a skit with the Mighty Carson Art Players or some other sketch, Johnny will rehearse. Otherwise, he goes back to work on the monologue, the development of future sketch ideas, and the booking of future guests.

By 3:30 the line outside Studio One on Alameda Avenue in Burbank has grown, probably beyond the night's seating capacity. Although the auditorium seats about five hundred, the number of tickets available to the general public varies from day to day, depending on the number of VIP tickets that have been requested by organizations and individuals, such as Carson Productions, NBC, sponsors, the State Department, and assorted TV producers and bosses. In addition, guests on the show often request tickets for their managers and friends. Sometimes as many as fifty or more of the seats are held for VIPs, though on a normal day about twenty-five are set aside. Curiously, VIPs, while seated well, are never given the best seats in the house. Those seats closest to Johnny are reserved for the people who have stood patiently in line on Alameda Avenue. It's Carson's own belief that the civilians, not the show-business industry types, are the ones who have made *The Tonight Show* a success.

Although most of the guests who will appear on the night's broadcast are in the studio by 4:30 and have, if necessary, rehearsed their musical numbers, they will not meet with Cason until they appear on the show itself. It's another of Carson's beliefs that meeting with guests beforehand somehow vitiates, no matter how slightly, some of the energy of the show.

Guests, looked after by their respective talent coordinators and a stage manager, sit quietly in a small room called, in time-honored theater tradition, the Green Room. Coffee, soft drinks, and occasionally a glass of wine are available to them there. The furnishings are modest: chairs and coffee tables. A TV monitor moans on with the local NBC broadcast until *The Tonight Show* begins. Then the guest, often growing more hapless and nervous, can watch the show progress, until the stage manager summons him or her to walk the few feet to the big curtain and wait for Johnny's introduction.

In general, guests are discouraged from drinking liquor before and during the show. Once Marlon Brando, reportedly in a high state, walked off the show; he is the only person ever to have done so.

But this rule has not always applied to Johnny and Ed, though nowadays their mugs are filled with soda water, tea, or coffee. In the late sixties Johnny's mug occasionally held a vodka and tonic, or a scotch and water. Ed's was reputed to be a punch made of various liquors from an old Lowell, Massachusetts distillery recipe handed down through the generations.

As the guests wait in the Green Room, Johnny sits in his office-dressing room, until about fifteen minutes before taping time. He is dressed in clothes from the enormously profitable Johnny Carson apparel line. His staff selects what Johnny wears, making sure that each item is currently available for sale in retail clothing stores. The clothes Johnny wears, however, are slightly different, specially cut to fit his own rather odd physique—a thirty-two-inch waist and a body builder's forty-two-inch chest.

At about five o'clock, Ed McMahon stops in Johnny's dressing room for a few moments. Carson sometimes shares a joke or theme with McMahon that might arise in the monologue, but

CARSON

Ed, whose laugh is genuine, never knows in advance exactly what Carson will say. Ed then heads off to join Fred de Cordova, Doc Severinsen, and a house manager. Together they "warm up" the studio audience. In the last half hour before the show, de Cordova will go back to see Carson for a minute-long discussion about details. McMahon and de Cordova are the last people Carson speaks with before appearing in front of the audience. And when they leave his office, McMahon rubbing his hands, and de Cordova, clutching the manila folder of notes he's about to place on Johnny's desk on the set, Carson is set for showtime.

At 5:10, the VIP guests are led into the auditorium of Studio One. In their excitement, few notice the metal detector and other forms of security. The set for *The Tonight Show* is much smaller than it appears to be on the television screen, only about thirty-five feet in length and width. As viewed on television, there are Johnny's desk and guest chair and couches; the stage where the monologue and acts are performed; and the bandstand, which is a steely bluish gray. In front of it is a large grand piano and in front of that a podium used by Doc Severinsen. This not only holds his music and cues for the night, but also often shelters props that Doc might use in the course of the show, along with an occasional and inexplicable stuffed animal. Doc also brings his dog, Lily Love, with him to the studio, but after the rehearsals, the pooch is consigned to a rear office.

At center stage embedded in the black floor is a white star, which is Johnny's mark—and only Johnny's mark. In television, the performer must stand at a certain place chosen in rehearsal, or risk appearing out of the picture. On most stage sets, the mark is indicated by a two-inch piece of masking tape. Johnny gets an embedded spot. In the auditorium, masking tape is stretched across the rows of seats reserved for VIPs. And as the VIPs come

34

in, they have their names checked against a list and then they are seated by one of the dozen or so NBC pages who work in the studio.

The Tonight Show audience is divided by two aisles into three sections. The two sections closest to Johnny are reserved for the pure civilians. The VIPs sit by the bandstand.

When Johnny does stunts like "Stump the Band" he never enters the VIP section, working instead with the civilians. When Johnny goes into the audience he has no desire to talk to agents and other show-business types. That explains why the VIPs are relegated to the far section and why Johnny never ascends the far aisle.

By 5:15, the VIPS and the ticket-seekers have all been seated.

Simultaneously, the stage managers and band members are filing into their positions and working about on the set. Band members tend to be jokey, and help in preparing the audience for the show.

While the stage crews make last-minute adjustments, the band members play loud, brassy music, and await the arrival of Doc Severinsen, de Cordova, and Ed McMahon.

In an interlude, a stage manager explains the ritual and etiquette of the show and answers any questions. Chief rules: no cameras and no yelling.

Although home audiences have heard studio audience members yell out to Carson from time to time, they don't see that yellers and photographers are escorted out immediately. Bulky security men, as well as a local cop or two, are on hand during *The Tonight Show's* taping, and they really do enforce the rules.

The most frequently asked question: When will the show taped today air on television? The answer: Tonight. *The Tonight Show,* though taped at 5:30 p.m. West Coast time, is broadcast the same day throughout the country. And although it's a taped broadcast, the tape is neither edited nor changed. A word may be blipped out, but the tape itself is never cut, nor is a scene reshot. *The Tonight Show* is as close to live television as one can come in a country with four time zones. In that it is broadcast unedited and as taped, it is a rarity among television shows, where retakes and retapes (even in front of live studio audiences) are the norm, not the exception. The fact that you can't stop the tape and "redo" a shot on *The Tonight Show* is, to most Hollywood TV actors, the scariest aspect of appearing on the show. There's no second chance, and most actors need seven chances just to walk through a door and find their mark, let alone open their mouths and speak coherently.

Preparing the audience of *The Tonight Show* for the actual taping of the show is the major job of the last half hour before taping. All television shows have a warm-up, or prep time, in which the audience, baffled by the cameras and unsure of what's about to happen, is briefed and encouraged.

While the house manager answers questions and warns the audience about yelling and snapping pictures, and the crew adjusts lights, producer de Cordova—natty this afternoon in a corduroy jacket, brown tie, beige shirt, brown trousers and brown shoes—arrives clutching the manila folder containing the biographical information and notes about each guest, which he places on Johnny's desk.

Then he walks past the guest chair and the couch and steps off the carpeted platform. At the couch, or the McMahon end of the platform, and just below it is a swivel chair of the same material as Johnny's own chair. This is where de Cordova will sit for the balance of the show. Next to him on a wall facing Johnny hangs a large clock with a second hand. While it's 5:20

Pacific time in the studio, the clock, which is both Johnny's and de Cordova's guide for the evening, reads 11:20. On the set of *The Tonight Show*, the illusion is that the time is the late-night broadcast hour.

Behind de Cordova is a small aisle leading backstage. Behind that and a few feet above de Cordova's chair is the show's control booth, a glass-enclosed room where show director Bobby Quinn sits with his assistants. It's from this booth that Quinn issues the instructions to the cameramen and stage managers below, and communicates with de Cordova.

Next to de Cordova's chair and almost in front of the couch is a hand mike attached to a stand. When de Cordova finishes placing his folder on the desk and consulting with a stage manager, he picks up the hand mike and walks over to center stage where he begins to talk to the audience.

"We're going to spend a little time together now; let's get to know one another. First, shake hands and say hello to the person directly behind you."

Everyone does, and de Cordova laughs, although he's done this same routine a thousand times before. He then makes a few mildly blue jokes about Doc and the band members, but nothing stranger or heavier than you might hear in the rec room of the neighborhood cut-up.

"Turning now," he says, "to the subject of tonight's show, we're privileged to have as a host a young comedian you've probably heard of . . . "

There is a small gasp from the audience at this point, and a few mumble words like "Jay Leno?" "Garry Shandling?" even "David Brenner?"

De Cordova continues, "And I think he's a comedian with a great future. His name is . . . Johnny Carson."

The relieved audience bursts into applause. Then, as Ed McMahon waltzes in from off stage, de Cordova introduces him and hands over the microphone. When we see Ed, dressed in a burgundy suit, standing there and holding the microphone, we realize we are watching the first of many familiar sights. Ed, in front of the couch, is in the same position we see him in every night at 11:30 when he introduces Carson.

Sounding like the amiable Atlantic City barker he was, Ed loosens up the audience by mocking Doc Severinsen's weird strut and yakking about the show about to take place.

But we are not the only ones watching Ed. From behind the familiar multi-colored curtains at stage center, Johnny Carson watches his old sidekick on a television monitor. Then, on cue, McMahon ends his patter. As the cameras begin to tape and the band's music starts to build, Ed begins his famous introduction to the show. The audience roars. Johnny, as he has done for twenty-five years, waits for three seconds, and then, through the part in the curtains, just as McMahon has promised, "Heeere's Johnny . . . ."

In front of us again, he is not merely an entertainer, he is not just a comic, he is our national humorist, sometimes even our conscience; at other times, just a late-night pal. Johnny Carson is a keystone of American popular culture.

But few people have ever known much about him.

2
Pie Plates
on the Roof

W hen I started working on this book, I had met Johnny Carson only twice. The first time was at the 1982 Oscar party given by the fabled Hollywood agent Irving "Swifty" Lazar following the Academy Awards, which Johnny had hosted on television.

Lazar's party is a not-to-be-missed rite of the Los Angeles year which attracts the socially correct of the movie business and Beverly Hills. Carson was in the crowd at the Bistro, a Beverly Hills restaurant that serves as a watering hole for the predators of Hollywood and Los Angeles. Wearing white tie and tails, accompanied by his then wife Joanna, he was seated at a table covered by a white linen tablecloth. Joanna, turned in her seat, was talking to a woman at another table. Whoever else had been sitting with them had left to mix with the likes of Gregory Peck, Jack Lemmon, Shirley MacLaine, Roger Moore, Teri Garr, and the studio bosses present.

Johnny's hands were crossed in front of him, next to half-full glasses of wine and water and an ashtray with a burning cigarette. He looked tired, as a man might after hosting the Oscar show, which had kept him on his feet for over four hours. He smiled slightly as a friend introduced us. He was shy and polite, and clearly not interested in small talk. I made my compliments and excused myself. Then, long before the other guests, he and Joanna left, presumably for home. On the night of the entertainment world's senior prom, he was homeward bound by 11:30 p.m.

His behavior epitomized what I had heard: that off-camera he was self-conscious and bashful. In that room of massive egos and flashy women, he seemed remarkably quiet. Uncomfortable even.

Then about a year later, I met him again at a party hosted on Superbowl Sunday by Pierre Cossette, an accomplished, lively, and social television producer.

Given at Chasen's, the other major watering hole of Beverly Hills, the crowd was considerably more sporty and informal than it had been at the Bistro. Steve Martin was there, along with Angie Dickinson, and other Hollywood regulars. Guests helped themselves to chili and ice cream and sat in front of outsize TV screens. In Chasen's huge kitchen, where the guests were serving themselves, Johnny Carson stirred a caldron of chili and chatted with a stunning California blonde. This time he was amiable, alert, eyes twinkling and full of jokes. He was the Johnny Carson his fans know and love, the Johnny Carson described by friends as being—"in real life"—exactly like the Johnny Carson viewers see on *The Tonight Show*. He made a couple of jokes about the press hype surrounding the Superbowl, but when he discovered the woman he was talking to was a member of the press—Martha Smilgis, then the bureau chief of *People* magazine—he smiled and walked immediately back to the dining room. He does not like the press. So he sat by Steve Martin and, for the rest of the afternoon, the boys traded jokes and loud, friendly laughter.

These were two personal experiences with Carson that piqued my curiosity. He was one of the most powerful men in the entertainment business, but an enigma, someone whose life behind the scenes was almost completely unknown, except to a few. Carson, in his monologue, could exert significant influence on politics, even the presidency. He could introduce others to great careers in show business. Heaven knows, he has affected the nighttime routines of millions of Americans. But who was Johnny Carson, the man to whom audiences had given such great power?

One was left to speculate on the basis of just tiny shards of information, and those glimpses of him in public: like the one at Lazar's party when Carson was formally dressed amidst the glamorous and mighty, and the other at Cossette's party where he was unusually affable (Carson, in the kitchen, ladled out chili to others, an act of common courtesy, something almost unknown among the stars).

As time passed, I began to wonder why no major book had ever been written about Carson (I looked). This was a fact that was highly unusual and very provocative. I wondered—not to be melodramatic—if there were barriers and perhaps dangers associated with looking into his past. In some ways he began to resemble another great mythic American figure famous for his vast influence and presence and his personal remoteness: Citizen Kane.

So I set out to learn about Citizen Carson, hoping that what I would find would be as entertaining and as interesting as the Carson who walks out from behind the NBC curtain.

First I went to his home town, far from Hollywood, in the Midwest, to see what clues Norfolk, Nebraska, far in the fields, might offer.

To reach Norfolk, which is in the northeastern corner of the state near South Dakota and northwestern Iowa, you fly or train or drive first to Omaha, 114 miles to the south. When the weather went bad in Chicago, while I was en route to Omaha, I changed from a plane to a train, taking the one daily train that carries passengers to Omaha from the east. Riding in the near-empty club car, I watched Johnny's monologue on my tiny portable TV as we crossed the snowy Iowa plains. The steward and the five other passengers came by to watch and laugh too.

From the railroad station in the old downtown section of Omaha, I drove off late into the night to a Howard Johnson's motel in a hilly, suburban section of Omaha. In the hotel bar, on this cold, late night, were just a few salesmen, a couple of solitary travelers, some women and men from the air force base, and a few rollicking members of a family group who had slid in from Purdum and Sodtown, to the west, for a shopping expedition the next day at the very close-by Westroads Mall, which they described as "the largest enclosed shopping center in the four-state region."

One sixtyish-year-old man, with a weather-worn, ruddy face, wearing jeans and a cowboy dress shirt, sat at the bar, puffing on a cigarette and nursing a beer. He had a small bandage on his left wrist and said he was in Omaha for some hospital treatment for a heart condition. He was a farm equipment dealer from, as he called it, "Fargo, Nort'dakota." When I told him—without telling him why—that I was heading for Norfolk, Nebraska, in the morning, he reeled back in his chair, and laughed and said:

"That's a great place. Norfolk. A real fun city. When I was a kid we lived halfway down below Yankton, South Dakota, out on the farms and we loved to go into Norfolk. A big city to us, but not too big. They had about ten thousand people then. It's double that now. They had a roller rink, with a wood floor and a tent for roller skating in the summer time. There was an ice cream place called The Palace, and a pharmacy, and a couple of theaters. They even had a cafe there that was open all night. And the telephone company office was there. They had operators on duty twenty-four hours a day; we used to like to go over and meet the operators coming off work at eleven at night and try to date them that night. Some of them did. A real fun city back in the forties. It still is today. Farm people move there when they've had it with the farms. It's always been the right size. We're still sort of scared of big cities like Omaha and big-city people. Norfolk people are nicer, but they're no slouches. They're sharp. Johnny Carson comes from there."

With all that in mind, I drove off the next morning in the snow to Norfolk. It was a long hundred miles. And until I reached Madison, just south of Norfolk, there wasn't even any radio reception—just static. Then the flat plains turned into hilly country, and at the crest of one bluff, a radio station from Shenandoah, Iowa, flashed on and off and then came in loud and clear.

But the Shenandoah station wasn't broadcasting music, pop or classical, nor was it airing evangelists, talk shows, or farm market reports. Eerily, the Shenandoah station, for the fourteen miles from Madison to Norfolk, broadcast a Jack Benny radio program from Easter 1943. This seemed an odd coincidence because Benny had a great influence on Carson. When Carson was young, he studied Benny's shows, and in later years Benny became a good friend.

For those last miles of my trip, Benny and Rochester railed away about life in Beverly Hills, and the script was very funny. Hydroplaning my hired Honda into Norfolk, past a sign welcoming me to Johnny Carson's home town, I was laughing out loud and marvelling at how good the jokes and sketches were, wondering if Carson, a high school senior when the show was first broadcast, had heard the show when it was originally aired. Then the Benny show faded away again into the ages.

But other elements that have influenced Carson also emerged. After checking in at the Best Western Villa Inn Hotel & Convention Center, at the corner of Omaha Avenue and South Thirteenth Street, I walked to the coffee shop and opened its foggy glass door. Looking up I saw before me a crowd of about twenty-five real-life variations on Johnny's wild hunting-behatted bumpkin TV editorialist, Floyd R. Turbo. As I sipped my decaf, the various Turbos groused long and loudly about hog-belly prices, the Iowa-Nebraska football game, the pinheads in Washington, the city people from Yankton and Omaha who were buying up the farms, and, of course, the weather.

Later I went over to the Sunset Plaza Shopping Center to buy a map. In the obligatory community room, a free cholesterol screening was under way. Among the participants were a number of women who could have passed for Aunt Blabby, enduring— with what no one would regard as silent stoicism—the pinpricks of the blood testers. One of the Aunt Blabby's hit one of the testers with her hefty handbag.

Norfolk (originally named North Fork because of its locale on the north fork of the Elkhorn River but renamed by a Post Office Department tired of forks, north or south) was settled around 1885 by German and Bohemian farmers who came from Wisconsin looking for new acreage. The arrival of the Chicago Northwestern Railroad produced the city, and the merchants followed soon thereafter. Today the railroad is still a major employer, but there's new industry coming in, as the townspeople proudly point out.

It is a typical sort of town, one which has demographics and values that make it the sort of place *The Tonight Show* aims for. Like most prosperous places it's full of churches and restaurants. In a quick drive around town, I found nine Lutheran churches along with churches for the Seventh Day Adventists, Baptists, the Assembly of God, the Catholics, the Christian and Missionary Alliance, the Church of God, the Church of Jesus Christ of the Latter Day Saints, and the Reorganized Church of Jesus Christ of the Latter Day Saints, the Congregationalists, the Episcopalians, on and on.

You can eat at Burger King, Dairy Queen, Diamond Lil's, McDonald's, and Jennie's Country Kitchen. There's also the Uptown ("An elegant atmosphere . . . where casual attire is welcomed. Cuisine that ranges from Novel to traditional"), Kentucky Fried Chicken, Mary's Cafe, and Ricardos I, II, and III, not to mention scores of others. Steaks and pork are staples on menus, and breakfast includes biscuits with cream gravy ($2.40 for bacon, eggs, coffee, and said biscuits). A hotel room rents for thirty-nine dollars a night. And there are apartments advertised for rent in the Norfolk *Daily News* for $110 per month. New homes start at about twenty thousand dollars even today.

Norfolk is a prosperous, pretty little town, then, of about twenty thousand people. Johnny's childhood home is in an older neighborhood—at 306 South Thirteenth Street—near downtown Norfolk. While the Carson home, now inhabited by a young family, is a neat, white, frame bungalow on a tree-lined street, today, the choicest neighborhoods in Norfolk are in subdivisions with names like Bel Air, Westridge, Western Heights, Woodland Park, Suburban Acres, Sunrise Additions, Crestview Heights, and Wedgeview. South Thirteenth Street is part of the past.

Although Norfolk, Nebraska, is Johnny's home town, he was born in Iowa, in a village called Corning, on October 23, 1925. While still a very young child, his family moved to Avoca, Iowa, another village. His father was a lineman with the local electric power outfit, a strenuous but flashy job for its time. Homer Carson, Johnny's father, was something akin to one of today's computer technicians—a hard worker on the edge of something new in American life. And as the utilities grew and developed through the rural Midwest, the elder Carson, known naturally enough as Kit, moved around as he took better jobs. When Johnny was eight, the Carson family settled in Norfolk (where Kit Carson would eventually become a manager with Consumers Public Power, now known as Nebraska Public Power).

Norfolk was, Johnny would later recall, "the biggest place I'd ever seen." He would remember that on the family's first day in town, staying at a brick four-story hotel on Norfolk Avenue, he stared out the window, marvelling at all the traffic moving along the street.

From the hotel, the Carsons—Johnny, his father Kit, his

mother Ruth, his older sister Catherine, and younger brother Dick—moved to the bungalow on South Thirteenth Street.

While the Carsons lived modestly, they did what they could for their children, including Johnny. At the depth of the Depression, his father had thirty-eight dollars for a top-of-the-line American bicycle, and when, at age twelve, Johnny wanted to send away to Chicago for a magic kit, the family had the few bucks for him to do so.

"It was a beginner's kit from a magicians' supply house in Chicago," Carson would later remember, "but it fascinated me. I spent hours learning the Amazing Dancing Cane and the Interlocking Rings. I was hooked."

With the magic kit, he graduated from trying to trick his sister into laughing at the dinner table when her mouth was full, to something more formal and ambitious. Until the magic box arrived, the extent of Carson's entertainment was self-entertainment, which included shenanigans like nailing a tin pie plate to the roof over his brother's bedroom to enhance the distracting sound of the rain. With the magic box, he found other and better ways to drive his family crazy.

He began to spend hours in front of the mirrors at home, practicing the Chicago tricks.

"To this day," says sister Catherine, now living in Monterey, California, "we get Johnny's goat by saying 'take a card any card.'" His mother, Ruth, recalled that family members weren't even safe in the lavatory. "Once I was in there," she said, "and he was on the other side of the door, yelling 'take a card, take a card.'"

Johnny's enthusiasm was encouraged, however, and in imitation of a travelling magician who had once sauntered through Norfolk, Johnny began to call himself "The Great

Carsoni." Mother was persuaded to sew him a magic cape, and as a teen-ager he delivered his first performance in front of the local Kiwanis Club for three dollars.

His obsessive devotion to show business at the expense of almost anything else would come later. Then he still had time for joking with the other kids. "Johnny was always fast with the lip," says a friend still in Norfolk. "He was kind of Irish in that way. Us Bohemian kids would just be sitting there saying 'duh!' while he'd be putting us down and sending us up."

Every urban neighborhood, especially in communities of new or relatively new immigrant groups, always has had one or two kids who were a little sharper, a little less rube-like than the others, and Carson was one of those kids. Carson still has these qualities which help make him so easily familiar to so many people today. Ask a stranger anywhere in America about Johnny Carson, and chances are that at one point he'll say Carson reminds him of someone from the old neighborhood, someone who was always ready with a quip.

As Carson grew older he began to use his wit for something other than magic and neighborhood jokes. A column in the high school yearbook entitled "Carson's Corn" went like this:

"Football season opened [this September] and I went out to make the team. I would have too if they hadn't found where I hid my brass knuckles . . . November was the month of blackouts, which the students enjoyed very much. December ended with Bob Jesson waiting at his fireplace for Santa Claus and bag. Bob was interested in the bag, I believe."

And Johnny's friends remember his nature and his humor. Recalls high school classmate Jack Hurlburt, now president of Mobile Premix Sand and Gravel Company in Littleton, Colorado:

"Everybody had their cliques. Eight or ten of us ran around

together. Johnny was a loner in some respects because he wasn't involved in athletics like the rest of us . . . .

"He was dedicated to his music, his drums, and his magic. Bob Reckert, Dean Wetzel, Johnny and I did a skit for the senior graduating class that was the forerunner of Karnak the Magnificent. Johnny wore a turban and masked his eyes. I hid under the card table and peered through the cheesecloth to see the audience. Bob and Dean were in the audience, and asked people to hold up articles that Johnny, through 'his mystic powers,' would then identify. I, of course, was the one who saw the articles and whispered the information to Johnny. We tore the place down when at the end I said, 'Hell, I can't see that.' Johnny came up with the idea. His talents were directed towards entertainment. You knew he would be an entertainer, even though he was an introvert and didn't show a lot of confidence in himself."

But John Franer, now an orthopedic surgeon in Cleveland, Ohio, remembers a different Johnny: "There was no way of knowing he was going to go on to become a national entertainment figure. He was shy down deep, even though he put on an outgoing appearance."

And other schoolmates have their memories.

Doris Kerlin, who with her husband owns a bicycle shop in Norfolk, remembers: "He was a fairly quiet sort. Of course, I was too. In school years ago they used to have assembly, and the whole school would come into this big auditorium, and we'd have different types of programs. Sometimes it was a guest speaker, sometimes school talent. Johnny did a lot of magic shows. My husband remembers Johnny giving a program in his home for some kind of church youth group."

Donna Goosen, now a registered nurse in Norfolk, who works

as the director of the student health department at the community college: "I remember him as being creative and funny. I was in some of his classes, history and government—that kind of thing. He was friendly and had a lot of friends. He was creative; he did a lot of writing for the senior annual. He wrote all the captions and the commentary. I don't remember a thing about magic shows."

Larry Sanford, another classmate, and now a stockbroker in San Francisco, with the firm of Donaldsen, Lufkin, Jenrette:

"John and I were good friends. He was more interested in magic and his shows and theater. We emceed a show together. He was always interested in magic. He was a ladies' man even then. Always going out with pretty girls even then.

"Johnny always found humor. If you read the yearbook you'd see he was tuned into what was going on. He wrote features for the yearbook."

"He was pushy and outgoing and had a need for public attention," remembers Gene Mauk, who runs Norfolk's Brass Lantern Restaurant, a boisterous, happy spot popular with the prospering and fun-loving of Norfolk (With friendly waitresses, good steaks, and generous drinks, it is the place where Johnny Carson held his fifty-ninth birthday party). "He was not much of a conversationalist. He was a performer. He used to do a soft-shoe routine for pep rallies. Johnny had the same type of humor then that he gets away with now."

"He's a very nice fellow," says Miss Fay Gordon, who was a teacher of Johnny in high school, and who keeps in touch with him even now.

"Not long ago I was in the hospital having a hip replaced, and he called me. He came from a very nice family.

"In school he was shy, and if you're with him even today he

isn't funny at all. He did magic when he was in high school. In those days they did pep rallies and oftentimes there would be a program and he'd do some magic. He did magic around school and town in the evening for an entertainment.

"I can't recall his best subject in school. I would say that he was probably a 'B' student. I don't remember his grades at all.

"He was too small to play basketball or football. He tried football but soon discovered he was too small to participate.

"He loved magic as a student. I had too many students to foresee what the future would hold for him . . ."

Carson's old friends describe a boy who seems to have been the father of the man. The high school cut-up, with his Carsoni the Great in turban and his Carson's Corn, presages the monologist and sketch-maker of today. His magic suggests he was smitten, even then, with show business, and his job (He was an usher at the Granada Theater—where he and the audience heard the news of the bombing of Pearl Harbor when the theater manager interrupted the show to tell them) might even suggest that he was taken with Hollywood.

But plenty of kids love these things though they never really pursue them. Why did Johnny? Part of the answer can be found in what happened to the other kids in his class. Many of them today, like the broker, surgeon, and businessmen quoted earlier, live elsewhere now, far from Norfolk.

"Norfolk," recalls Larry Sanford, now of San Francisco, "when we lived there, was an agricultural town. You could have had parents who had a large business, but if you didn't and weren't a farmer, you had to look elsewhere, if you had any drive at all. The opportunity wasn't there. Most of us went into the service, and then afterwards it was a question of 'How you going to keep 'em down on the farm, after they've seen Paree?' I was introduced to San Francisco during the service. I was in the air corps and fell in love with the area. I think something similar happened to a lot of us from Norfolk."

For Johnny, Norfolk was a happy place, where he was well-loved by his family, and encouraged to develop his odd interest in entertainment and magic. His childhood was by no means sad or unhappy. No horrible hurts urged him to show business. Some simple love and the interest and understanding of his townspeople allowed him to know what he liked to do, and that he was good at it.

And the economics of Norfolk, today a pleasant, thriving town, also helped him by forcing him out. It was then a small town without much opportunity.

As teacher Fay Gordon, now ninety, who has lived in Norfolk since the twenties, puts it, "How many people do remain in their home town? They go to university, and whatever their chosen field, they have to find work wherever that is in that field." Miss Gordon brings up another belief that Norfolk thrived on (and still does): the value of schooling. The war may have called all these midwestern kids, but their parents drummed into them the importance of higher schooling. Johnny may have liked magic, but he was taught to get that degree as well.

Soon after his high school graduation, Johnny went into the service, and Norfolk would never be his home again.

3
Carson's Cellar

Before enlisting, Johnny embarked on an adventure, a storied adventure, one so laden with implications about his future, that some have wondered if the escapade might not actually be legend. But Johnny insists all the events really happened. As the story goes, and as Kenneth Tynan recounted it in the *New Yorker*, Johnny, shortly after graduation, hitchhiked to Hollywood. "I had to go," he's been quoted as saying. "I wanted to see the place."

Hollywood then was doing its best to entertain the hordes of servicemen then passing through town, but it was interested only in entertaining servicemen, not gangly high school graduates. So Johnny, allegedly, donned the uniform of a navy midshipman, and made his way to the Hollywood Stage Door Canteen and other hot spots.

"I danced with Marlene Dietrich," he has said, and one night—or maybe it was the same night—he went to San Diego to see a magic show. When the magician asked for volunteers from the audience, Johnny's hand shot up. On stage he "ecstatically permitted himself to be sawed in half."

The magician, according to Johnny's story, was none other than Orson Welles, the celebrated movie maker and amateur magician, who later became a frequent guest on *The Tonight Show* and a friend of Carson.

Johnny's tale of his Hollywood adventure ends with his being arrested by the shore patrol for impersonating a midshipman, and being fined fifty dollars.

Afterwards, he did enlist in the Naval Air Corps, and went south for training. Not mixing well with the program, he transferred to a naval officer's training program based at Columbia University in New York City.

"I came out of that an ensign," he recalled, "and was assigned to the battleship *Pennsylvania*. The war ended while I was on the way to the ship, which was in Okinawa.

"The *Pennsylvania* had been torpedoed the day before we got there; they practically blew off the stern and killed twenty guys. She headed into dry dock at Guam. I was assigned to damage control; I guess maybe because I was the youngest officer and the most recently arrived.

"My first assignment was to go down into that hole in the stern and supervise the bringing out of those twenty corpses. They had been down there eighteen days and I want to tell you, that was an awful job."

His next task was less harrowing. Several months later, after the *Pennsylvania* had sailed to Seattle, Carson was assigned to be commander in charge of a train full of homeward bound veterans. The slow train wheezed across the plains states, and at one point halted for many days in the snowbound Dakotas. "It was another incredible job. I did my best but those guys had their own agendas."

Months later, when he was working in Guam as a communications officer, Carson had a chance encounter with Secretary of the Navy James Forrestal, who was on a tour there. One sleepless night, Forrestal started a conversation with Carson, who was on duty. Forrestal asked whether he planned to stay in the navy after the war. Carson later said he thought of fibbing but, instead of flattering the boss, told the truth and said no.

Forrestal then asked just what his career plans were, and Carson, perhaps surprising even himself, told him that he wanted to be a magician. Forrestal responded by asking Carson to perform some magic. For the following few hours, Carson entertained the insomniac secretary of the navy with card tricks learned in front of the mirror at 306 South Thirteenth Street, Norfolk, Nebraska.

For Carson, what was most important about this experience was his discovery that he could entertain and amuse someone as cranky and sophisticated as Forrestal. He had a sense he could handle audiences somewhat more demanding than the friendly members of the local Kiwanis and 4-H clubs. To make a Washington politician laugh was something of an achievement.

So in early 1946, when he was honorably discharged from the the navy, he left thinking that maybe there was a future for him in show business. His family, believers in education, encouraged him to take advantage of the education benefits available to veterans. So he enrolled at the University of Nebraska, located in Lincoln, also the state's capital. In this he was typical of his Norfolk classmates.

"Most of the fellas," says former schoolmate Doris Kerlin, "when they came back from the war went on to school on the GI Bill. Some fellas went to school and settled in areas of the country where they had been stationed. A lot, like Johnny, came back home and went to the University of Nebraska."

At first, he majored in journalism, with the idea of becoming a comedy writer, but after a few months he switched his major to speech and drama, with the more daring idea of becoming a radio performer.

Roommates at the Phi Gamma Delta house, themselves veterans, who shared the fraternity house at 1425 "R" Street in Lincoln, found that after the first few months Carson changed from being just another undergraduate to something else: an incredibly hard worker, but a distant one.

Jack Hurlburt, his classmate at Norfolk High, after three years in the army also returned to Nebraska and the state's university.

"I was a Delta Tau Delta," Hurlburt recalls, "and Johnny was Phi Gamma Delta. We double dated. He was very intense. Not outgoing. Sometimes he went off on his own where a lot of us spent time together."

At first Carson tried to fit into fraternity life, but like many returning veterans, he found aspects of college life and the Greek social system silly, though Carson did write for the Awgwan, the campus humor magazine and participated in Kosmette Club Shows—these organizations were modeled after the Harvard Lampoon and Harvard's famous Hasty Pudding Institute (which would name Carson man of the year in 1978).

Carson, however, was focussed on making a living and a career for himself. One of Johnny's moneymaking activities was described by a college classmate to *TV Guide* in 1966. "Gasoline was still rationed," the classmate recalled, "so Johnny rallied us to build up a good business. We pooled our gas-ration stamps, and we supplemented our supply through various devious means—don't ask how—and we sold gas in beer bottles at fifty cents. Obviously, a fellow couldn't get very far on a beer bottle of gas, but at least he had some mobility, and it took him and his girl to a quiet parking place.

"Then our stamps ran out and our other sources dried up, but Johnny had an inspiration. He had a jalopy that had finally collapsed, and he didn't have the money to buy parts to repair it, so we all towed the car back to Phi Gam house where, of an evening, it was very dark, very quiet. Johnny rented out the car as a necking parlor for twenty-five cents an hour and did a rushing business. Privacy was guaranteed."

Soon, though, Carson had a real job, an adult's job, working for Radio Station KFAB, writing for a western comedy show called *Eddie Sosby and the Radio Rangers*. "Carson got up at five in the morning to do the radio show," recalled Norris Anderson, a fellow fraternity member. "He was a very industrious guy, working several jobs and his tail off."

His brother Dick, four years younger, was already an undergraduate at the university when Carson returned from the service. Dick Carson recalls that Johnny was eager to move on.

Johnny had two targets: getting a radio show of his own and making it as a magician. And to that end, he rehearsed his magic constantly, inviting a girl from North Platte named Jody Wolcott to be his assistant. They met in 1948 when he was emceeing the University of Nebraska women's show called *The Follies*. Jody and Johnny would marry in 1949, and would be divorced in 1962.

Jody, who now lives in a western state, gave her first interview for this book. She remembers her early days with Johnny, whom she always refers to as John, in this way:

"John and I met in college," recalls Jody. "I was in my junior year. I have a B.S. in fine arts from the University of Nebraska. I was a cartoonist on the weekly campus magazine. I was a Pi Beta Phi, and John was Phi Delt. I was John's assistant in his magic act. In fact those were our dates; he never had any money for a real date. He made twenty-five dollars for the evening. We'd go to milkmen's conventions, fairs, whatever. Finally, I was expelled from my sorority because I wasn't keeping hours.

"So I went to live with my grandparents—my grandfather was the head of the biology department at the University of Nebraska, and my grandmother worked at the college. My parents' home was in North Platte, home of Buffalo Bill."

And at the campus radio station, Carson was eager to do anything he could. At one time he participated in an experiment with a new toy called television. He played a major role in a program about bovine disease entitled *The Story of Undulent Fever* which was broadcast all the way from the studio in the cellar of the building to the top floor, almost fifty entire feet away. They say the camera loved him right from the start.

The key fact of Carson's undergraduate years was in his constant, ambitious work. "He was in front of the mirror for hours at a time," recalls a former roommate, "and he was a chain smoker. He was a driven guy. And he was driving us crazy."

He prepared a thesis for his degree entitled "How to Write Comedy Jokes." An unusual project, it was taped, not typed. Carson's thesis consisted of a compilation of jokes and skits from prominent and popular radio shows of the day, interspersed with Johnny's running commentary on the comedic technique. It was a good thesis which helped Carson to graduate in three years, not four. But Carson did not forsake all extracurricular activities for work and study. He and his assistant in the magic act became engaged. Though Jody had her own interests, including continuing as a cartoonist, Johnny and she were married in 1949, moving into a seventy-two-dollar-a-month apartment in urban Omaha, where Johnny had a job waiting as a station announcer on radio station WOW. During the summer months, Jody moved back to a family summer cottage near North Platte. Johnny has fond memories of driving out there after work on the weekends.

"Jody's family had a nice cottage out there by a lake, and when I finished work at the radio station about 1:00 a.m., I'd speed up there. The major highways in Nebraska are straight and wide, with no traffic. I could easily cover the distance by dawn. She'd usually be there waiting for me by the lake, and both looked breathtakingly beautiful in the sunrise."

He was hosting a forty-five-minute morning radio show which from all reports was offbeat, even if the persona of the announcer was on the self-inflated side. *The John Carson Show* was billed as offering the "tops in music, interspersed with John's inimitable chatter."

The chatter may not have been inimitable, but by Omaha standards it was positively urbane in its appeal. Omaha morning radio, then as now, was devoted to lengthy and necessary farm reports, with thorough discussions of the prices in all the midwestern markets for beef, sheep (shorn and wooly), pork bellies, and cattle (on and off the hoof). Alternatively, there was network radio. Originating in New York and Los Angeles, it was pompous and as distant culturally as it was geographically. But Carson's humor was immediate, personal, and refreshingly skeptical—very different from the farm news and the network shows—and listeners liked it.

Then as now, his humor extended to the sponsors of the show. In one celebrated incident, he nearly lost his job over comments he made about a local thrift institution known, to itself anyway, as "the friendly bank."

"Drop in any time," quipped John (he was too young to be known as Johnny, a name that suggested someone even younger). "Drop in at two or three in the morning. That's fine. Help yourself. Leave a note." Well, that may not be a knee slapper, but it was enough to create a furor, and it garnered for Carson the reputation as a nonconformist.

His willingness to tangle with established authority extended to WOW management as well. As the story goes, once a zealous station auditor demanded payment of twenty cents for one of Johnny's personal phone calls. Carson ignored him for months, until the auditor threatened dire action. Carson then spent twenty-five dollars to hire an armored car complete with gun-carrying guards to personally deliver Johnny's check for twenty cents to the auditor. (In later years, Fred Silverman, when he was president of NBC, would also learn that Johnny could be extremely stubborn over issues of money and control.)

Carson's nonconformity, however, also made him eager to try a show on WOW's new TV station, which was then broadcasting to about thirty-five Omaha homes, a couple of taverns near the Union Pacific station, and the TVs on display in L. Brandeis's Boston Store emporium. Called *The Squirrel's Nest,* the fifteen-minute show broadcast at 3:00 p.m. was at once a precursor to the monologue section of today's *Tonight Show* and a zany homage to Fred Allen's radio shows, which were made up of both wit and comment. On, or rather, in *The Squirrel's Nest,*

Carson mused on the events of the day, life in Council Bluffs—the Iowa city across the Missouri River that was to Omaha as Brooklyn is to Manhattan—the vagaries of the Nebraska unicameral legislature, and the behavior of bureaucrats in the utilities—a subject on which he had learned a lot from his hardworking but independent-minded father.

At one point, however, the *Nest* was abandoned by its sponsor who apparently felt that Carson's material, especially his jokes about castor oil, were on the adolescent side.

As a response, Carson grew the first in a series of beards—which have come and gone throughout his professional career—and announced he would refuse to shave it off until the *Nest* was occupied by another sponsor. Within hours the phones were ringing with support for Carson, and within two days he had another sponsor. The beard came off.

Carson would go on to host other shows on WOW, creating comic characters and, as usual, gathering as much experience as he could. Among these shows was a children's program entitled *Uncle Ank and Andy*. In later years, Carson would use this experience as the basis for his nightclub sketch about the miserable Deputy John and his adventures as a horribly hungover kid's show host. These early shows also produced the prototype of the wicked-tongued Aunt Blabby.

Richard "Pete" Petrashek, who is now the chief videotape editor at WOW-TV in Omaha, was an office boy when Johnny first came to work there.

"Johnny worked at WOW radio," says Petrashek, "as a deejay and as a general announcer in 1950. Our television station had just gone on the air in August 1949, and Johnny came up to the TV station to do station breaks—thirty seconds in between programs.

"Because of his personality, the TV people put him on live shows. He did *The Squirrel's Nest* and was sort of a host to short film programs like the *Our Gang* comedies. Every five or ten minutes he'd cut in and do a magic trick. He was also a ventriloquist. If he wasn't doing magic or ventriloquism, he'd interview somebody like a fireman who had saved somebody's life. And he was the host of several other different shows. He did *Coffee Break* where he'd invite guests in and they'd talk over coffee. It's like what they do today on shows like *Hour Magazine.*

"He was also a newscaster on radio and maybe on TV once in a while. His main job was as morning disc jockey on radio WOW. They had the highest ratings of any radio program. Johnny was innovative and had a great sense of humor. He worked for WOW for about two years in total. He came right out of college. I think he was hired by Lyle de Moss, a showman and emcee who was then the program director. Lyle also booked Johnny on the side doing freelance magic shows. Johnny and I did card tricks together at the station.

"Radio was still in its heyday then. The stars came through town on tours, and we'd book them on our station. Jack Benny was Carson's idol, along with Fred Allen. Johnny was a born comedian. He was always 'on' and ready to make a joke about something.

"When Johnny left here, he had no job in Los Angeles, as I remember. He said he thought opportunities would be better in Los Angeles. I know he worked in radio out there first, and managed to get around. I heard he knew Red Skelton went to a certain restaurant. And from what I heard, he sat in a booth in the restaurant with some friends and did an imitation of Red Skelton doing a seagull imitation, and then Red introduced himself. That's what I heard.

"Johnny did everything at WOW. He did stand-up routines, jokes, and patter. One time he did something on the *USS Missouri* when it got stuck somewhere in the mud. He did a little routine in which he posed as a newsman saying, 'We sent a diver down to see what's the matter.' He'd say, 'We've got Charlie down there in his diving suit. What do you see, Charlie?' Then [Carson would] put his head in the wastebasket. And as Charlie he would say, 'Well, I guess we're in sixteen feet of mud.' Then Johnny would say, 'Here comes the captain, Admiral So-and-so. Admiral, looks like you got stuck in the mud. How did that happen?' 'Well, just lucky, I guess,' he'd respond. We had about a million listeners."

Mrs. Lyle de Moss, whose husband was WOW program director, remembered Johnny this way. (Mrs. de Moss also spoke for her husband, who had been ill.)

"When Lyle was program director at WOW, Johnny would come out to our house, and I remember once he climbed up on the roof. He was messing around with the pigeons. I heard someone knocking on the picture window, and I looked, and there was Johnny upside down on his stomach, his face against the window.

"We used to see him around because Lyle also booked him to do freelance magic tricks. Just local things around town.

"He was a nice boy. He was shy, real thin, and had coal black hair. He wasn't as attractive as he is now."

Carson has contended he did not understand why he was unhappy in Omaha. Married since 1949 and a father since 1950, he was successful and well liked, making more money (fifty dollars a week) than he thought he'd ever be making. Yet, in 1951, he began to feel that he should move on. He not only was chafing under the restrictions and constraints of management, but he

63

also believed that in larger cities, radio and television management would recognize and appreciate his talent. Had he known then that entertainment management, everywhere and in every clime, often consists of people who won't and can't recognize talent, he might have given up. But he did not, and early in 1951, he began making an audition tape for other stations to listen to.

Along with a friend, Carson and Jody put together thirty minutes of the twenty-five-year-old Carson doing everything from topical commentary in the Will Rogers style to local public service announcements and commercials. The idea was to wow them outside of WOW. On his two-week vacation period in 1951, he took the tape and travelled to every radio and TV station he could find in California, covering all of them in Los Angeles and San Francisco, along with a fairly good percentage of those in between. "You've got to make your own breaks" was the adage he followed.

But the trip was a disaster.

At most stations, personnel refused either to listen to his tape or even interview him. Repeatedly, Carson was left to cool his heels in scores of waiting rooms, only to be told there were no openings and that no one was interested in talking to him. Nevertheless, there was one small break. An old friend, Bill Brennan, was working in Los Angeles as a salesman for the CBS radio and television stations, KNX and KNXT-TV. Brennan, out of friendship, prevailed on station officials to listen to Johnny's audition, which they did. But at the time, they sent Johnny home only with their thanks and a promise to call him if ever there were an opening.

Carson was totally disheartened by his audition trip and convinced that nothing would come of his efforts. But, about *five months* later, Brennan phoned Carson in Omaha: There was an opening for a job as a general station announcer, broadcasting time signals and station identification announcements. The type of work represented a major setback for Carson, but the job was in Los Angeles, and the pay would be $135 a week. Carson, who saw the position as a step in a larger plan, accepted.

Leaving Jody and son Chris behind until he found a home, Carson set out for Los Angeles in an old car with a rental trailer.

"When I finally got there," Carson recalled, "I looked like something out of *The Grapes of Wrath* driving down Sunset Boulevard. Everything that could have gone wrong with the car had gone wrong, and I was a wreck."

Carson's job as an all-purpose announcer had Johnny sitting in a soundproof booth for much of the working day, watching a clock and a cue schedule. He was merely a voice carrying out a job usually done by older, sleepy hacks, or human calliopes who found endless satisfaction in the sound of their own phonic trilling.

To any ambitious performer, a job like Johnny's must have seemed like the end of the road, and in fame-and-fortune-conscious Hollywood, such a job marked Carson as a virtual nonentity.

Los Angeles is a city where what you do is what people regard you as being capable of doing. Advancement is seldom given easily. If you're a station weatherman, it is practically impossible to convince a producer that you're capable of being, say, a game show host, which is a story that Pat Sajak, the host of *Wheel of Fortune*, could tell. And to most people, though probably not to Johnny, his prospects seemed dim.

After finding an apartment in a suburb called Toluca Lake, near Burbank, he sent for Jody and their baby. When they arrived, after she had a chance to size up their situation, Johnny promised Jody and himself that he would have his own television show within a year, or else.

At first, the best he could do to rise above the routine work was the occasional task of introducing network programs to the United States. But by sheer persistence, at year's end, he got himself a fifteen-minute show on KNXT. "The station [managers] finally gave him the show," says a friend, "to get him off their backs. He was an incredible pest, always asking for the show, always asking everyone." The station management didn't realize, as his parents and those who had to endure years of "take a card, any card" did, that persistence was a hallmark of Johnny's life.

Jody, his first wife, now feels this was "the most interesting segment of his life . . . of all his lives. After we moved to L.A. and when he was working as a disc jockey and he also did his magic show, he was home a lot and spent a lot of time with the boys. I helped him with his scripts. It was a lot of fun. We left Nebraska in 1951 and went to California. We lived in four different places there and finally had a lovely home."

His show, *Carson's Cellar,* was broadcast at 4:00 p.m. on Sunday afternoons, in TV terms a throw-away time slot that could safely be given over to a beginner. With a production budget of twenty-five dollars a week, the set was a simple one, consisting of a counter-length podium and some chairs. Typically, the show would present Carson doing his zany commentary on current topics, followed by parodies of other television shows. Though Carson only got fifty dollars a week for his effort, his work was an investment that paid off. In its thirty weeks on the air, the show gained quite a following, especially among people in show business, largely because of the fun it poked at TV. Once, a horde of girls, almost indiscernible individually, raced back and forth in front of the screen to mock the then popular penchant for huge production numbers. Another time, Carson announced that Red Skelton was the show's "special guest star." A lone figure then raced across the stage. That, Carson said, was Red Skelton.

As fortune would have it, at that moment Red Skelton was in his Beverly Hills home watching Carson's show, and he burst into laughter at the mockery of the guest-star spot. He called Carson and agreed to appear, in a relatively stationary form, on the show for free. Soon other big comic stars like Jack Benny and Fred Allen were making appearances on *Carson's Cellar.*

Carson's lousy time slot on Sunday afternoon was a kind of blessing. The big comics of the day, busy during weeknights with their own shows and guest appearances, seldom had a chance to watch television themselves except on weekends—particularly on Sunday afternoon, when Carson was sending them up. Liking what they saw, they became fans.

Ira Cook, a retired Los Angeles disc jockey, remembers the *Cellar* show as a famous one. "Johnny had lots of big names on the show—like Milton Berle and Red Skelton—but they were always messing around; he never seemed to actually perform with them or get anyplace with them." Nonetheless, the show was a hit, while some of Johnny's other early ventures into television were not.

From 1952 to 1953, Cook himself was one of the host disc jockeys on a Sunday night Los Angeles television show called *Platter Panel.* It was popular with, Cook says, "the beach crowd," the same crowd that had flocked to the radio shows done by a disc jockey named Steve Allen, who had become so big that by 1953 he was in New York hosting a popular late-night local television show called *The Tonight Show.*

Platter Panel, says Cook, "was similar to another big show called *Hit or Miss* where disc jockeys played *new* songs and people voted on them.

"We played *old* songs and people voted on them. We had a special panel of celebrity guests who did the voting. Under a big, funny host named Frank de Vol the show was itself a hit."

In 1953, however, de Vol was replaced by the ambitious try-anything host of *Carson's Cellar.*

"Johnny was really talked about by Hollywood insiders," says Cook, "when he was on *Carson's Cellar.* They said he was fantastic. But on *Platter Panel* people didn't seem to like his humor. Only four months after Carson took over, the show was cancelled.

"I guess Johnny just didn't fit into our type of show. His humor was too subtle, I think. Frank de Vol had a great sense of humor and a big smile, and Johnny would make a joke and then a funny expression, the way he does today. Only today everybody loves it.

"At the time he was so young," Cook recalls, "he was like a kid.

"One night [a few months after the show was cancelled] I ran into Johnny and his wife having dinner at The Ram's Head restaurant in Encino, in the Valley. I asked him what he was going to do next. He said, 'Boy I've had it with this town. I'm going to New York and work there, and if I don't make it, I'm going to sell shoes.' "

It would be a long while before he went to New York, however. He would first take and leave a number of jobs, including one as the host of a show called *Earn Your Vacation.* It was so awful that Carson still won't talk about it. With the success of *Carson's Cellar* well behind him and a number of failures still fresh in people's minds, Carson did manage to get a job with Red Skelton, who had taken a shine to him. But Carson had to give up being an on-air personality, or "talent," as they call the watchables. He would work behind the scenes as a writer.

Carson did much of the Skelton writing, concocting silly skits and jokes, and he might have stayed a writer much longer, except that during the rehearsal for the show of August 18, 1954, Skelton, falling through a prop door, broke his leg and was forbidden to go on. In desperation, the show's producers called Carson at his home and told him in the legend-honored show-business fashion that he would have to substitute for the stricken star. He hastily wrote some material and drove to the studio, trying out his his lines. He opened the show with a monologue that began, "Personally, the way I feel right now, I think Red's doctor should be doing the show." He was a smash. And the critics, both in the papers and in the profession, raved about him. Then when Jack Benny began talking him up around the network, the executives listened. And in July 1955, Johnny was given, at age 29, his own network show as a comic.

Apparently at the zenith of his career, with his highest ambitions achieved, Carson with his wife Jody, who worked on the show as a singer, appeared on the cover of the September 3, 1955, issue of *TV Guide*, sipping a soda. Things looked good, but they were bad.

He had gone from being an anonymous voice on KNX to being a smash substitute for a TV star to being a nationally known personality overnight. That was the good part. The problem was that Johnny was not allowed to take charge of the show. He tried, but he was far too flush with sudden success to realize that he needed to call all the shots, not just write and perform in the skits.

Every CBS exec with a working voice box had a different idea of what to do, and each of them had a say in the program. The result was a *Johnny Carson Show* which featured lavish production numbers with dancers and balloons, when in fact the star was a guy who worked best when low key and alone. The sketches he wrote, like parodies of popular TV shows and a roving reporter bit, worked well for him, but the total package just didn't click.

Charlie Isaacs, who was head writer of the show which was sponsored by Jell-O, has these memories: "CBS gave Johnny a break, putting him, a new performer, on the air. He didn't have the power he has now. He was just happy to have a show. Now he controls the show [*The Tonight Show*]. Then Ben Brady, the producer, controlled the CBS show, and I think there was always a little friction over that."

Brady said to *Life* magazine, "Carson was trying to be a major comedian in prime time, and he didn't have the power. It was that he didn't have the experience; he is generically not a strong stand-up comedian like Hope, Skelton, or Benny. He wasn't then, he isn't now, and he never can be." Others remember it differently. Says Isaacs, "Johnny did pertinent monologues, better than today's. [One well-known bit] was on Princess Grace's wedding. He said, 'Everybody is interested in this wedding because everyone likes to see a little girl who has everything get the rest of it.' He did sketches, satires on current events, costume sketches like one on Alexander the Great.

"The show was a better-done *Saturday Night Live* with more cohesion. They didn't dub in laughs either. The show was on for an hour—at 6:00 p.m. on the West Coast and 9:00 p.m. on the East. He was very good. It was Johnny's timing and his facial reactions that were so great. That's what made him funny. He did a lot with his face.

"He wasn't like a Jackie Gleason or a Sid Caesar. We put him into situations where he responded. Johnny is very good at comment comedy. After *The Johnny Carson Show*, I didn't work with him again until I did a season on *The Tonight Show*."

The first major newspaper review of *The Johnny Carson Show* appeared in Jack Gould's *New York Times* column on July 8, 1955. Gould wrote: "The Columbia Broadcasting System may have a comer in a young man named Johnny Carson, who now has his own show. He is a humorist of the quiet, unhurried school, and he has a most engaging smile and personality. With help, he could go places.

" . . . What Mr Carson [has] is a singular, youthful charm, and an impish twinkle in the eye. He seems like the proverbial nice guy down the block. To capitalize manifestly on this asset is the CBS assignment; last night Mr. Carson was not fortified with sufficiently strong material or an adequately competent supporting company.

"The best part of the show was Mr. Carson's delivery of a report on the teen-age problem, which included the statistic that there were 27 million boys and girls who were in absolutely no trouble last night. The country's high schools, he further suggested, were becoming nothing but breeding grounds for education. It is this sort of line that Mr. Carson can throw away effectively.

"The rest of the show, unfortunately, was only too typical of summer video fare—a routine girl vocalist, a conventional jazz unit and a sketch about a guest who did not know when to go home.

"CBS might well be advised to give Mr. Carson more inspired directorial guidance and brisker scripts. He would seem worth the investment if only because he is such a warm and pleasant individual on the home screen."

Time magazine, in a short piece that featured a photo of a flustered Johnny in sports shirt and trousers, scratching his neck and holding a cigarette, reported: "The most promising and engaging personality on the summer replacement circuit is Johnny Carson, twenty-nine-year-old star of CBS's *The Johnny Carson Show*. With a droll sense of humor, Carson never raises his voice but has an effective way of raising an eyebrow, and he combines a slow double-take with quick smile. Given good material, he could be irresistibly funny."

The mannerisms that attracted those critics thirty-one years ago are still the ones that appeal to us today. But they were buried in the program.

From the outset Johnny's show, rudderless and directionless, was a disaster. Writers and directors were changed almost weekly, and morale was low indeed. Managing to complete his scheduled run of thirty-nine weeks (then the norm in television), Carson was cancelled on March 28, 1956. The following week the Toni Company, makers of women's hair care products ("Which twin has the Toni?") took the time slot over from the Jell-O people and brought America *The Arthur Murray Party,* featuring those two punishers of parquet, Kathryn and Arthur Murray.

But as others danced on, Johnny, despite a contract with CBS, couldn't find work. In a very short time, he had gone from the realization of his own Omaha dream to oblivion. For the next year, he was virtually unemployed and unemployable. At one point, he took a nightclub act out on the road and found himself booed in such places as Bakersfield, California. And the first strains on his marriage began to appear. His family then included not only Jody and their first son, Chris, but also his second and third sons, Ricky and Cory.

To get his career moving again, Johnny looked for a new

manager—someone who could get him jobs in television. Finally he met Al Bruno, a manager who not only had extensive contacts in the television business, but also was said to specialize in re-starting stalled careers.

Bruno thought there was a place for Johnny in television, but that place would be in New York, where all the major decisions were made and much of the programming in television was still done.

Bruno knew hundreds of the vaudevillians, active then in TV, who were able to book his clients as guests on game and variety shows. He urged Johnny to head east and join the Friars Club, a kind of Elks Lodge for successful entertainers, lawyers, and producers. It was a place where Johnny could get to know people.

Johnny knew he had to go, even though he didn't have the money to support a move to New York. He had to borrow $2,000 from his father, who was more than happy to help the son who liked to be a showman. With the borrowed cash (including some advanced by Al Bruno) in his pocket, Johnny headed east, leaving behind Jody and the boys. He was on his way to the *real* television land, far from its outpost in Hollywood.

4

Guests Shots, Best Shots, A Marriage Falls Apart

I n New York, Johnny hung out at the Friars Club when he wasn't auditioning for full-time jobs on every game show being cast. He also made guest appearances on any show that would have him, appearing on *The Ed Sullivan Show,* for example, in September 1955—but playing his drums, not as a comedian. Allan Funt, recalling Carson's audition for a job as host of *Candid Camera* said, "I thought he was terrible." For Johnny, it was an up-and-down existence.

"Carson made himself well known around the Friars Club," remembers one ancient habitue of that spot. "He was a very amiable kid, even if he didn't fit into the crowd of old-timers from vaudeville, burlesque, and radio. But no one could fault him for trying. He was out all the time going after work. He'd try out as a host, as a comic, as a straight man, as an actor, as an announcer, as anything. He was very hungry. I don't know that the Friars Club was ever much help to him, but he's been a loyal member ever since hitting it big. Very charitable guy. He must remember the hard days well to be that way."

Eventually, one of his auditions did pay off. He was hired to host a game show. In 1957, the ABC network was just beginning its effort to broadcast programming during the day (as distinguished from the evening prime-time hours), and it wanted a lively, offbeat show which would draw attention away from frothing soap operas and goofy children's programs. Don Fedderson, who was the producer of the show ABC chose entitled *Who Do You Trust?*, has explained its origins.

"The show was originally a nighttime production called *Do You Trust Your Wife?* and the emcee was Edgar Bergen. The quiz show scandals knocked off all audience participation shows even though we were really clean. So the show went on daytime on ABC, and I went looking for a new host.

"One of the people we considered and liked was Dick Van Dyke. But the staff liked Carson who also auditioned, and even though the director hadn't been a big fan of *Carson's Cellar*, Johnny was hired—for about five hundred dollars a week.

"The first three months were touch and go from show to show. But in six months his confidence was there and the show worked. We gave him top writers and producers, including a guy named Art Stark.

"We rehearsed the shows with dummies and fed Johnny the lines. It was the appearance of the real people, the real contestants, that made for the spontaneity. We did as many as three shows a day, and while the show started in 1957 with modest ratings in the beginning, by the time Johnny left in 1962, it had hit ratings of about thirty, a highly respectable showing." And by the time Johnny left the show in 1962, he was making $2,500 a week as the host.

In some ways the show resembled the current *Tonight Show*, a fact which has led some to claim that the real genius behind Johnny's success is not Johnny himself, but the man who produced *Who Do You Trust?*, Art Stark.

Stark developed a format in which the guests were not the usual nerds who were found on quiz shows. Stark sought out oddballs and eccentrics with offbeat hobbies and accomplishments. The humor of the show came from the pre-quiz interviews that Carson did with his guests about their hobbies. The quiz portion of the program, as was also the case in Groucho Marx's *You Bet Your Life*, was almost irrelevant. *Who Do You Trust?* was less a game show than it was a talk show posing as a game show. Talk shows just hadn't been invented yet. Carson's lines, sometimes scripted, sometimes ad-lib, made the show work. Some examples:

A body builder who was a contestant once cautioned Carson to respect his own body, "the only house he'd ever have."

"My house is pretty messy," Carson retorted, "but I have a woman come in once a week to clean it out."

Another time a woman contestant spent eleven minutes of air time trying to teach Carson how to breathe through his toes. "I almost got the hang of it," Carson said, "but my left big toe was stubborn, or maybe just stuffed up that day."

And once two flea-circus operators came out and put their performing pests through their paces while explaining, in response to Johnny's question about how the insects ate, "We just put them on our arms and they nibble away, buffet style."

77

Other guests solicited for punishment on *Who Do You Trust?* included a man who had delivered a mattress via the New York subway, a lady wrestler who married her judo student, and a man whose claim was that he was a "firster": the first across the George Washington Bridge; the first on the New York Thruway; first on the Triboro Bridge; and the first to drive through the Holland Tunnel.

Stark may have had the right notion to combine interesting eccentrics with a witty host but the success of the show was due to Carson. His own ad-libs were often funnier than those written for him, and he frequently veered away from the prompted questions into his own areas. *Who Do You Trust?* became Carson's show. It was no accident that, as more and more television shows moved to studios in the West, Carson's show stayed in New York, adhering to the New York standard of television, which was "Make it interesting, and it'll be good," while the westward bound shows adhered to the Los Angeles standard of broadcasting which was, and is, "Make it look good, and it'll do fine." Carson, having endured the chaos of Los Angeles TV with its emphasis on looks over content, found himself right at home in New York where interesting content, not gangs of dancers or car crashes, were regarded as good TV. He also happened to like New York.

"Today," says a long-time associate of Carson, "the *Who Do You Trust?* stuff seems silly, not very engaging, and Johnny, in retrospect, appears not to have acted on his ambition during those five years. He was still ambitious in many ways. But he also was enormously relieved to have a secure income and a show where the format was settled and in concert with his own instincts.

"The CBS year had driven him crazy, having to live through a parade of directors and producers, each with wildly different ideas of what the show should have been. Those were miserable days. The *Trust* years were in some ways calmer. Art Stark knew what he was doing, and Carson worked well with him and with the format. There was no constitutional crisis every day. They both knew what to do, and so long as the guests kept on coming in, they knew the show was a hit and would stay. In many ways, that was a great relief to him. He was very appreciative of what Stark had done in providing and sticking to a format that both of them knew made sense.

"But Carson was not Stark's dummy. It wasn't a case of hiring *anyone* to do the show. If that were the case, *Who Do You Trust?* would have been a hit after Johnny left. It wasn't. The new host's name was Woody Woodbury, and no one's ever heard of him since."

Like most TV shows of that era, *Trust* was performed in a converted Broadway theater and Carson, who had made many contacts at the Friars Club, continued to move among the Broadway types who then dominated television. Not surprisingly, he had other job offers. In January 1958, while Johnny was still the host of *Who Do You Trust?*, he opened on Broadway replacing Tom Ewell for some weeks in the Broadway run of a very slight romantic comedy entitled *Tunnel of Love.*

He took a few acting roles on television as well. In 1960, he appeared twice on the prestigious *U.S. Steel Hour* in very light comedies. One, virtually forgotten, was called "Queen of the Orange Bowl" and co-starred Arlene Francis. In the other, entitled "The Girl in the Gold Bathtub," Carson received more attention. He had a featured role as a hip advertising man.

Critic Harriet Van Horne, then of the *New York World Telegram,* spoke of Johnny as having a "nice, amiable Stover-at-Yale charm," but the show itself induced a case of the vapors in the formidable Miss Van Horne, who is still reviewing television in New York, having survived the collapse of many newspapers.

"The plot was fairly fresh," she wrote, "and might have been interesting if treated tastefully." She said the story involved an advertising agency's search for a solid gold bathtub, with Carson as the account executive.

"For Johnny Carson to emerge from the contessa's bedroom," scolded Miss Van Horne, "in a white chiffon negligee was a cheap and monstrously vulgar touch. So was the business of his being slugged and falling into the bathtub. (And unconscious bodies crumple before they stiffen, someone should advise the director.)"

Johnny did no more dramatic or comedic roles on Broadway or on television (though in 1964 he appeared in movie, entitled *Looking for Love* with Connie Francis, George Hamilton, and Paula Prentiss). In fact, Carson was discovering that one did not have to be a serious actor to be serious—or successful—in show business. Carson's kind of television was coming into its own. And Carson was getting better at it; his instincts for the camera were beginning to sharpen. It was during these years that he began to develop thoroughly those fantastic Oliver Hardy takes, the Jack Benny pauses, and the Huck Finn blushes.

When he arrived in New York, Johnny had established his wife Jody and their three boys in a New York suburb called Harrison, near the Connecticut line. It was to have been the family home.

But Carson was soon spending most of his time in a small apartment in Manhattan's Yorkville section, a once German neighborhood of brownstone houses, then becoming the neighborhood of choice for people working in midtown. It was by no means an expensive neck of the Manhattan woods.

What had happened in the Carson marriage is something that is not entirely clear. Jody, according to some reports, had become

Johnny in one of his first publicity photos, circa 1953, Los Angeles.

*Johnny in one of his most recent
publicity pictures, circa 1986, Los
Angeles.*

Jack Benny was one of Johnny's first fans, and when Johnny was still trying to break into the big time, Benny invited him to appear on his program, where this picture was taken in 1954.

In 1954, while Johnny was working for Red Skelton as a writer, Skelton broke his leg, and the young Carson "subbed" for him. This led to Johnny's ill-conceived first network show in 1955.

The endearing Carson mannerisms were already part of his act on CBS's Johnny Carson Show.

Surrounded by the "Carson Cuties" in 1955. The Johnny Carson Show *had lavish production numbers and no direction; it was cancelled after thirty-nine shows, and Johnny was out of work.*

Johnny and first wife Jody Wolcott. She was a Nebraska girl who fell madly in love with a magician. They were married in 1949 and divorced in 1962.

Johnny, Jody and their three boys—Cory (1½), Ricky (3) and Chris (4)—at their home in Encino, California, in 1955.

Although his own game is tennis, Johnny's is the most famous golf swing in America.

Johnny and Joanne Copeland at their wedding in 1963. It was the second marriage for both of them.

Enjoying the high life in New York with Joanne. Truman Capote and David Susskind were their neighbors at the U.N. Plaza.

Vice-President Hubert Humphrey, making an appearance on The Tonight Show *in 1966, was one of the scores of politicians who have found a welcome and a serious atmosphere on the show.*

The unforgettable wedding of Tiny Tim and Miss Vicki on The Tonight Show *in December 1969 scored huge ratings and hordes of reviews attacking the show's "tastelessness."*

After his second divorce, Johnny was seen out with many of Hollywood's most attractive ladies including actresses Jill St. John, Dyan Cannon, and Angel Tompkins.

Being a good sport, or at least a willing sport, has always been part of Johnny's job. Here he and Pele, the Brazilian soccer superstar, try some footwork.

In 1971, New York Mayor John Lindsay and Mrs. Anna Roosevelt Halsted presented Carson with a plaque for some good deeds for emotionally disturbed children.

Johnny and Joanna Holland, the former New York model, on the town in 1971. They were married in 1972 on the tenth anniversary of Johnny's hosting of The Tonight Show.

Johnny's parents, Homer and Ruth Carson. They bought him his first magic set and always believed in his capabilities as an entertainer.

Homer and Dick Carson, Johnny's father and brother, attending a Friars Club tribute to Johnny in 1974.

disillusioned and disappointed with the collapse of her own show-business career. And Johnny, still embarrassed and humiliated after the rough year of virtual unemployment, supposedly found home to be an unpleasant and tension-filled environment.

Then there were stories of problems in their lives individually—stories of stress and depression in Jody's life, stress and heavy drinking in Johnny's. Whatever it was, it seems that what did happen in their marriage is typical of the career confusions and personal tribulations that bright, energetic people often find themselves facing in their thirties. The future hadn't worked out quite the way they'd expected and each seemed to have personal demons and difficulties to face. The result, sadly, was that the marriage failed. Miss Fay Gordon, Johnny's former teacher back in Norfolk, reports that it was generally believed the marriage broke up because Jody wasn't able to keep up with the life and schedule of a game-show host in Manhattan. Johnny himself has said that he regards the collapse of his first marriage as his single worst failure.

When asked what went wrong with her marriage, Jody told us, "There are things you don't talk about. Basically, what went wrong was we had three children right away—the diaphragm was all they had in those days—and there was no money. It happens all the time to a lot of people.

"Women were always a problem but that went with the territory I figured. If you [are] married [to] someone in the public eye, women are constantly throwing themselves [at your husband], and beautiful women at that . . . and if your wife is pregnant out to here, well. Here, he marries this cute coed, and she is out to here all the time, and there's no money and no help . . . but it wasn't that different from other marriages really.

"The divorce was very hard. After all, we had three little boys.

81

It was a terrible thing. Suddenly, there I was alone in a house with the boys . . . . We separated in 1959, I remarried in 1970 and was separated about two years later. One of the main reasons I remarried was that I felt it would help me keep the boys. John and I had joint custody but he and Joanne were trying to get full custody. There really was no reason for it. Joanne let it be known in a *Ladies' Home Journal* interview that she had fixed up their United Nations Plaza apartment with the express idea of having the boys there. It was so unfair. The boys, as usual, were caught in the middle. Naturally, they responded to being wooed . . . but I don't think they wanted to live there.

"John always said publicly that the divorce was his fault, but he didn't really think this. I wanted a divorce, but he wouldn't give me one.

"But finally he said, 'You can have your divorce . . . .'

"He had someone meet me there in Mexico . . . I don't know who it was. I only stayed overnight. It was very quick and very hush-hush. I didn't know what was happening. I was very upset and overwrought. I arrived at night and a man met me and took me to a motel room. The next day the man took me to a dinky little office. Someone asked me some questions and then they put me on a plane."

Nowadays Jody says of the marriage, "I was the homemaker, the mother of his children. When I was married to John, I couldn't do anything outside the home. He wouldn't stand for it, but I didn't have the time either. Those were the forties and the fifties. I would have liked to continue as a cartoonist . . . .

"I've just finished reading *Men Who Hate Women* . . . and I think I've figured it out. What's wrong with men is their egos— and this is especially true with men who are celebrities or entertainers. I married two of those. They were both very creative, very artistic, and very verbal—and the second was quite a performer in his own right too. My conclusion is that men with very large egos just can't stand the competition with a woman— they want to dominate her. The great majority of men are egotists. I used think this was only true of men in show business but now I think it's the norm . . . .

"Men have this need to assert themselves by dominating their wives. I don't feel I was unassertive in our marriage but I was busy and pregnant all the time . . . . With Johnny, I started out very assertive but by the time it was over, I had lost it."

In telling her side of the story of their marriage, Jody was diffident about talking about Johnny. "People," she said, "don't want their heroes tarnished by other people . . . . No one wants to hear about tarnished heroes.

"The thing people don't realize is that they only see him five days a week on camera for just a few hours, and he is on stage giving a performance just like any other performer." Joanna Carson, Johnny's third wife, echoes this same theme in her story of that third divorce.

Johnny spent less and less time at home in the suburbs before and during the separation; he was mostly in Manhattan. Jody spent more and more of her time at home coping with three lively boys. Nevertheless, Carson, considering that he lived apart and worked unusual hours, was still able to be an attentive father, making a manly effort to look after his boys and their interests. According to a family friend, he spent more time with his sons than did many a more conventional father.

Neighbors remember the boys as rambunctious and prone to pranks, not unlike their father, who had in his own youth organized illicit school assemblies and spewed odd smelling odors through the school heating system; the sons themselves were given to tricks and escapades. One neighbor in Harrison recalls that in 1959, shortly after the Russian sputnik rocket forced everyone's attention on outer space, the Carson boys, with a homemade rocket, launched several local mice into partial orbit over the New England Thruway.

"They were very lively," the neighbor recalls, "and Jody often seemed to have her hands full. But they really weren't any more trouble than other kids in the neighborhood. They just were paid more attention to because of who they were.

"Jody's existence was very suburban and typical of the time. She busied herself with school and community activities and with keeping up the house. I think she missed her life with Johnny, but she never complained about that, and never complained about him either. It was clear that the marriage just didn't work out, and that was sad, and she was doing her best to be a suburban matron. Nowadays, she might have been able to go back to work. People around Harrison did feel badly for her, but I never thought she felt badly for herself. At worst, when her hands were full, she was distracted. But she was a valiant woman. We liked her for that."

Johnny's life in Manhattan, built around the *Who Do You Trust?* show and the very unsuburban life around the theater district and the advertising world, was hip and urbane and perhaps excessive, but it was fun and attractive too.

At times things were out of hand. Often, when three shows had to be completed on the same day, Carson and Ed McMahon, who had been hired as the announcer on the show, would spend the long breaks between shows in Sardi's, the celebrated show-business hangout, quaffing, in Carson's delicate and comic phrase, "a flagon of the grape."

The third show of the day, done under vinous conditions, was often inadvertently hilarious. On one such show, Carson could not remember what questions he had asked his guests, and repeatedly asked them time and time and time again, "Where are you folks from?" A friend from those days says, "I don't think Johnny really enjoyed those escapades. But the stress of the show and of the breakup of his family seemed to be bothering him. When he kept asking, Where are you from?, it seemed to me he was asking himself, Where am I going? He was funny, and busy and seemingly happy, but he was troubled. I don't think he knew that." Johnny himself has referred to this period of his life as his days of wine and roses in reference to the bittersweet Manhattan days of the bibulous and kindly character portrayed by Jack Lemmon in the movie *Days of Wine and Roses.*

Jody's recollection is harsher: "You'll find out to this day, he's not all that welcome in certain nightclubs in New York."

By 1961, *Who Do You Trust?* was near the height of its popularity, and to most people Johnny Carson appeared to be a success. He had, relative to most Americans, a tremendous salary ($2,500 a week), and he was a hipster, a man about town, seen squiring glamorous women through what passed for glamorous nightlife. But, as could be glimpsed when Johnny hoisted the flagon, there was an underlying tension and unhappiness in his life.

After a while, the nightlife was no longer exciting, and though a success, his career had plateaued. He *was* a network game-show host, but his career had yet to receive national attention, and Johnny was far from becoming a part of national consciousness.

He needed, like most people in their thirties, a chance to grow again. And luck, as he knew, was what you made of it. The luck of Johnny Carson would begin to improve on May 26, 1958, when he took an evening's gig as the substitute host for a show that once had been called *Broadway Open House.* By 1958, it was known popularly to millions as "The Jack Paar Show." Its real name was *The Tonight Show.*

5
The Tonight Show's Early Evenings

A lthough Johnny Carson has been hosting *The Tonight Show* for a quarter of a century, the show's origins are even older. Johnny is the best, but by no means the first, host of *The Tonight Show.*

Its precursors were a network program, *Broadway Open House,* and a local New York program with Steve Allen called *Tonight.*

Broadway Open House was distinctly New York in flavor. With roots in radio, vaudeville, and the Friars Club roasts, it began in May 1950 and ended in August 1951. Presenting Jerry Lester and Morey Amsterdam as alternating hosts, and a cast of regular guest characters, along with visits from Broadway and nightclub performers, the broadcast aired from 11:00 p.m. to midnight (there was no 11:00 p.m. news in those days). Early on, the show demonstrated it had an audience, helping to launch the sales of new songs and the careers of new performers. But conflict among the performers stopped the show from developing. Soon Amsterdam quit, and the program was airing only a few nights a week. Then Lester was replaced by comedian Jack Leonard, who wanted his own gang of regulars. By August 1951, the show was off the air, and the NBC affiliated stations were left to fill the late-night time period on their own.

Though short lived, *Broadway Open House* established a general outline for late-night programs to come, presenting the format of a regular host, a regular cast of characters, visiting guests, music, and sketches.

Another twenty-two months would pass before even the NBC affiliate in New York would try a late-night show, because no one in management seemed committed to making the late-night hour work. But finally another program was created, at the behest of a New York brewery, Ruppert Beer, which was interested in advertising on late-night broadcasts. The affiliate and the sponsor decided to use the *Broadway Open House* format. But a new host was brought in—someone who had been a great success on radio in far-off Los Angeles.

In June 1953, Steve Allen began to host the new show. Called *Tonight,* and sponsored by Ruppert Beer, the show aimed to do what Allen had done as a late-night disc jockey in Southern California.

Allen had built a huge following in California as the host of a radio program with a difference. While on the air Allen would leave his turntable and, with microphone in hand, go up and gab with his studio audience. (Originally the show had no audience, but listeners started coming by to see Allen.) The skits and humor were breathtakingly spontaneous—refreshing in an age of staged and stagy radio programming. When the NBC executives in New York, spurred on by the eager brewers, grew interested again in late-night programming, Allen was their man.

Allen's local *Tonight Show* continued in the casual California vein. The show began with Allen at the piano, offering notes, musical and satirical, about the news of the day. After ad-libbing, he frequently went up into the audience or out in the street to talk with civilians. He had guests, regular and irregular, and the show was soon a big hit. But only in New York.

Meanwhile, an NBC executive named Sylvester "Pat" Weaver (now also famous for having fathered actress Sigourney [*Alien*] Weaver), charged with the mission of expanding the network's broadcasting day and, thus, its revenues, was thinking about late-night and early-morning programming.

Weaver came up with a number of ideas for shows, including an idea for two versions of the same kind of show. One version, to be broadcast early in the morning, would be entitled *The Today Show*, the other, to be broadcast late at night, would be called *The Tonight Show*. At the outset, each had much in common with the other; it was only over the years that they would diverge. Each show would be heavy on the light and would also feature news. Gene Rayburn, more famous lately as a game-show host, was the news announcer on the original network *Tonight Show*. The news segment, however, was quickly dropped from the generally comic show.

In early years, *The Tonight Show*, just like the current version of *The Today Show*, was network owned and operated, not star-run. It may be that hosts on early-morning television were sleepier and less hungry than their night-time competition, but the hosts of *The Tonight Show* were considerably more rambunctious personalities. Not only did the network experience rough times with them, it found it expedient, more than once, to sell the show—lock, stock, and barrel—to its host, and then rent back just the finished program from him. Even though the show in its many variations was the brainchild of Pat Weaver, a network executive, it would eventually become the property—not just figuratively—of its stars.

Weaver spoke of his memories of the show not long ago in an interview: "*The Tonight Show* which originally ran for 105 minutes a night from 11:15 p.m. to 1:00 a.m., was born to make money.

"We were able to sell time that had never before been sold on television. The idea was: to sell this marginal time; to introduce smaller advertisers to network television by letting them put in a one-minute ad and letting them see how successful it could be; [to provide] a place to create and develop new stars, especially young comedians; and to provide a new form of competition to the late movies on television."

It was, he also said, designed to be a "coverage show," one which, like *The Today Show*, would acquaint viewers with the latest in entertainment and news. So, on September 27, 1954, with a cast headed by Steve Allen, Gene Rayburn, and orchestra leader Skitch Henderson, the formerly local *Tonight Show* moved over to the network and began broadcasting nationally.

Also featured, as the show developed, were two new young singers named Steve Lawrence and Eydie Gorme, along with another unknown singer named Andy Williams. Allen also assembled a cast of comedy regulars who played a variety of crackpot characters including Tom Poston (now George the handyman on *The Bob Newhart Show*), Don Knotts, and Louie Nye. In addition to a first-rate cast, the sketches and stunts were outrageously zany. Allen once persuaded the U.S. Marine Corps to simulate an invasion of Miami Beach, which caused a panic among startled civilians who assumed the worst. The show was so successful that the network mavens, in their constant quest for more, decided to launch a version of the Allen show on Sunday nights in prime time against the highly rated *Ed Sullivan Show.*

When the Sunday night show began, Allen continued to host *The Tonight Show* from Wednesday through Friday, with Ernie Kovacs taking over the first two days of the week with his own cast and format. But the viewers did not tolerate the changes well; ratings declined, and by January 1957, the first of the network *Tonight Shows* was over, to be replaced by a show closer in format to that of *The Today Show.*

Called *Tonight! America After Dark*, it was a disaster, lasting for only six months. At first hosted by Jack Lescoulie, formerly of *The Today Show* and then in its last month by one Al "Jazzbeau" Collins, *Tonight! American After Dark* was short on comedy and long on commentaries delivered by newspaper columnists from across the country. No one today will take credit for the benighted notion that talking newspaper columnists could be as interesting and as popular as Ernie Kovacs or Steve Allen.

When it became apparent that *Tonight! America After Dark* was a bomb, the network decided to return to a format similar to Steve Allen's original show. After finding out that Allen was not interested in a return engagement, NBC began a search for a new talent. Finally, they hit upon a young announcer-news reader from CBS named Jack Paar.

Network brass had all sorts of ideas as to what Paar should do with the show—none of them even remotely related to what he did do. Some wanted him to follow the fast-and-crazy format of Allen; others wanted him to turn the ninety-minute show into a program of three sequential quiz shows. Others suggested he do the news. Paar soon had his own ideas.

"I certainly needed the work," he has recalled. "I was assigned the leftovers from the previous shows. They were perfectly nice people, but [they] were not at all creative. I take little credit for suggesting and finally insisting that the only answer was to invent a conversation show. So my claim to fame is that all I did was to rearrange the furniture and introduce a davenport.

"I soon discovered that I was good with people [on the air]. I had a naturalness, even a feistiness and an honest curiosity about most things. I was a good listener and interested in what people had to say until they bored me and the audience . . . . The program was described then as one hour and forty-five minutes of people sitting around trying to change the subject. I called it 'a night light to the bathroom.' "

Paar, like Allen, relied on a cast of regulars including Elsa Maxwell, the famous hostess; Cliff Arquette (grandfather of actress Roseanna Arquette) as the rustic Charley Weaver; Hans Conried; Peggy Cass; Buddy Hackett; Alexander King; Genevieve; Betty White; and Pat Harrington, Jr. (more recently famous as the janitor on *One Day at a Time*). Harrington appeared on Paar's show as a mysterious character called Guido Panzini, the spiritual grandfather of Father Guido Sarducci, Vatican gossip who frequently appears with Johnny on today's *Tonight Show.*

Aired from July 1957 to March 1962, and broadcast in its early years from an old Broadway theater, this *Tonight Show* was an astonishing nightly assembly of talking heads—but it had people riveted. Half the time the audience was trying to figure out if Paar's guests were for real, and the other half they were trying to figure out if Paar was. In addition to Guido Panzini and

Charley Weaver, the show also introduced viewers to New York at its hippest, featuring guests like Judy Garland, Tallulah Bankhead, various Kennedys, and Albert Schweitzer.

By 1960, Paar was also enmeshed in politics, flying off to Cuba to interview Castro, planning trips to Moscow, and promoting his pal, Richard Nixon. Yet for all his important, strange, and intriguing guests, Paar himself was the main attraction. One viewer, who described Paar as "a minister after four martinis," said he watched only to see what Paar would do next. "He was so emotional—he'd weep, he'd hug, he'd drive you crazy. It was very popular barroom viewing."

In 1960, an episode involving a joke had him off the show for a month. The program had moved from Broadway to studios in the NBC offices at Rockefeller Center and was no longer "live" but videotaped. This gave NBC censors a chance to review the show before broadcasting. On February 11, 1960, Paar told a long three-minute joke, which the censor cut. Paar disappeared in protest. Eventually, the network persuaded him to come back, but this conflict was the first of a series of fights with individuals and organizations ranging from columnist Dorothy Kilgallen to TV host Ed Sullivan to the network brass to the White House to the Soviet Union. Finally, exhausted, he left the show on March 30, 1962, but not before helping the network pick his successor. He recommended Johnny Carson.

The joke that started Paar's long slide off the show is innocent by today's standards, but is still intriguing to many. Here it is:

"An English lady, while visiting Switzerland, was looking for a room, and she asked a local schoolmaster if he could recommend one to her. He took her to see several rooms, and when everything was settled, the lady returned [to England] to make final preparations to move. When she arrived home, the thought suddenly occurred to her that she had not seen a W.C. (water closet, or in American, a toilet) around the place. So she immediately wrote a note to the Swiss schoolmaster asking him if there was a W.C. around. The schoolmaster was a very poor student of English, so he asked the parish priest if he could help in the matter. Together they tried to discover the meaning of the letters *W.C.*, and the only explanation they could come up with was *Wayside Chapel.* The schoolmaster then wrote the English lady the following note:

Dear Madam:

I take great pleasure in informing you that the W.C. is situated nine miles from the house you occupy, in the center of a beautiful grove of pine trees surrounded by lovely grounds. It is capable of holding 229 people and is open on Sunday and Thursdays only. As there are a great number of people and they are expected during the summer months, I would suggest that you come early, although there is plenty of standing room as a rule.

You will no doubt be glad to hear that a good number of people bring their lunch and make a day of it, while others, who can afford to, go by car and arrive just in time. I would especially recommend that your ladyship go on Thursday when there is a musical accompaniment.

It may interest you to know that my daughter was married in the W.C., and it was there that she met her husband. I can remember the rush there was for seats.

There were ten people to a seat usually occupied by one. It was wonderful to see the expressions on their faces.

The newest attraction is a bell donated by a wealthy resident of the district. It rings every time a person enters. A bazaar is to be held to provide plush seats for all the people, since they feel it is a long-felt need. My wife is rather delicate, so she can't attend regularly.

I shall be delighted to reserve the best seat for you if you wish, where you will be seen by all. For the children, there is a special time and place so that they will not disturb the elders. Hoping to have been of service to you, I remain

Sincerely,

The Schoolmaster

6
A Paar of
New Shoes

I n 1962, when NBC first offered Johnny Carson the chance
to host *The Tonight Show*, he declined. The show, he felt,
was so closely identified with its mercurial and controversial
host, Jack Paar, that any successor would certainly be doomed
to die because of the constant comparison. The cool, slightly
blue, Johnny knew he was no feverish Paar. As author Gael
Greene would write later, "People [watched] Paar in sick
fascination for fear we'd miss a happening. [Paar's] insides kept
gushing out all over the studio floor . . . ." In complete contrast,
"Johnny Carson's just folks. Everyman. Midwestern.
Wholesome. Healthy and not overly involved. Not too smart
alecky. Not too prudish and not too dirty. Never too provocative.

Never controversial. Never sloppily emotional. Never too dull. Really just folks."

That a low-key personality would succeed in the *Tonight Show* spot seemed unlikely to Carson, but the network kept on pursuing him.

"We wanted someone like Paar," recalls an old NBC hand, who now chooses to remain anonymous, "but not completely like Paar's personality. Although the show was done from New York and was full of New York hipsterism, it was really being produced for the Midwest.

"Paar was a midwesterner, and when it came time to look for a replacement we looked for another midwesterner. Carson was really the only one. Plus there was the fact that Paar himself suggested Carson. Some of Carson's managers at the time tried to take credit for the idea of Johnny as the host, but really the idea came from Paar and from the network. We didn't expect, however, that he would turn us down."

Johnny made it clear to NBC that he didn't think he could replace Paar. The network, in a panic, told Carson that he could redesign the show and make it more his own. "We told him," says the old NBC-er, "that he could do his own show. We weren't interested in having him turn into Jack Paar; we were interested in the fact that, although Johnny was different, he had a similar appeal. I don't know if that makes sense, but we thought it did. We thought he appealed to the Midwest and that, like Paar, he was good with people on the air."

These discussions were taking place at a difficult time in Johnny's life. He was, at times, continuing to be kind of a hellion in Manhattan. "When Johnny Carson drank, he was not a very good boy," recalled Irving Mansfield of those days in the early sixties. Mansfield, along with his more famous wife, author

Jacqueline Susann, who wrote the steamy best sellers *Valley of the Dolls, The Love Machine,* and *Once Is Not Enough*, were regulars on the Manhattan nightlife scene. Mansfield recalls one night especially in the days before Carson began hosting *The Tonight Show.*

"We were having dinner one night at a very elegant New York restaurant . . . . We nodded to Rocky Graziano . . . and to Johnny Carson who was with his wife and some friends. Jackie had enormous admiration for Carson."

But, according to Mansfield, Carson came over to the Mansfields' table and sat down, conversing only with Irving, and ignoring Jackie. When Mansfield, aware of the slight to his illustrious wife, tried to get Johnny to include her in the conversation, "Johnny moved his chair and over his shoulder said something to Jackie that she did not like at all . . . . Jackie got into a rage and said, 'How dare you!' He growled at her. She threw her drink right into his face. He got up as though he were going to punch. I grabbed him and said, 'Come on, Johnny, watch your step.'

"In a way I felt sorry for him. He didn't even know what the hell he was doing. That's how drunk he was . . . .

"The captain came over. Rocky Graziano came over. I didn't want to see a fight between Johnny and Rocky. Johnny's wife, his second wife Joanne, and a waiter walked him out of the restaurant."

Later Jackie Susann, graciously and rather magnanimously, insisted the incident never took place, or at least not in the way it was reported in the press. But Mansfield's account, published after his wife's death, is regarded as the accurate "inside story." On another occasion, at the Copacabana in Manhattan, Johnny became so uproarious during a performance that the nightclub's public relations man and other staffers had to escort him to an upstairs office to rest and calm down. Recalls the P.R. man, "He was blind drunk and was heckling the performer—I think Don Rickles was on stage. Finally, we decided enough is enough and took him upstairs and let him take a nap."

The early sixties was not the easiest time for Johnny, and his mood may have had something to do with his reluctance to move from game-show host to successor to Jack Paar. But eventually he was persuaded to take the job.

"I suppose," he said at the time, "that I could be a lot safer by staying and doing what I am [hosting *Who Do You Trust?*]. After all, I'm making a hell of a good living [$2,500 a week then]. But I would like to try something a little more creative."

Joanne, his wife at the time, was said to be a big part of the decision. Joanne, who now lives in Bel-Air not far from Joanna, Johnny's third ex-wife, was herself a TV personality in the small world of New York TV before she met Johnny in March 1960.

Joanne told us, "We were introduced by my father, a businessman-lawyer with the Bechtel Company, who had met Johnny previously at a dinner.

"I was born and grew up in California, and went to school at the convent school of San Luis Rey in Oceanside and at San Mateo College.

"I went to New York in 1955, but had worked in TV in San Francisco earlier. And it's true I had been an airline stewardess before that and briefly had been under contract as an actress at RKO Studios. It was Howard Hughes who put me under contract there. But when I met Johnny, I was co-hosting a CBS program in New York called *Video Village*."

They were soon dating steadily and Joanne says they became

"buddies." Her new pal, though, differed from previous beaus in that he was becoming a star.

"I knew I was pretty," she said, "but I didn't think I was beautiful. Yet people kept looking my way. Once I turned to Johnny and said, 'Everybody is staring at me. Is my slip showing or something?' He became quite embarrassed, turned red, and said, 'I think they're staring at me.' That's just when I realized he was a well-known personality."

On a hot August afternoon in 1962, the two were married in Manhattan's Marble Collegiate Dutch Reformed Church. Johnny's brother, Dick Carson, was the best man. Also in attendance were Johnny's manager-agent, Al Bruno, and Johnny's producer, Art Stark—hardly surprising since no star would leave his agent and his producer out of a wedding. They're upset enough that the bride isn't one of them.

NBC had been considering a number of other different candidates for the job of host of the new *Tonight Show,* among them Groucho Marx and Merv Griffin, when Carson let them know he'd take the job. NBC agreed and hired Johnny at $100,000 a year. He was to replace Paar when Paar's contract expired on March 30, 1962.

There was just one hitch. ABC, which had Carson under contract until October 1962, wouldn't release him. The day after ABC refused to do so, Carson opened his broadcast of *Who Do You Trust?* with the words, "Welcome to ABC, the network with a heart."

ABC wouldn't budge, however, and a few days later on the show, when a yoga expert had maneuvered him into a painfully contorted shape, Johnny squeaked out at the camera, "Who's responsible for all this? ABC?" The network made him stay until October, which had two curious results. One was a sequence of

Tonight Shows from April to September that were hosted by an array of other TV stars. Many of these substitute hosts were undoubtedly hoping that Johnny would get stuck in that yoga position permanently. Second, there came an endless amount of speculation in the press about how Carson would do succeeding Paar, which could be responsible for Johnny's now famous dislike and distrust of the press.

Instead of guessing about how Carson would do as Paar's replacement, the press might have paid more attention to the weird *Tonight Show* of the interregnum, which featured hosts as varied as Art Linkletter, Bob Cummings, Joey Bishop, Jerry Lewis, Groucho Marx, Donald O'Connor, Jan Murray, Soupy Sales, Mort Sahl, Steve Lawrence, Arlene Francis, Jack E. Leonard, Hal March, and that famous duo from New York radio and television, Peter Lind Hayes and Mary Healy—many slavishly imitating Jack Paar. Meanwhile, Carson was using all his free time from *Who Do You Trust?* trying to come up with a new format for *The Tonight Show.*

A favorite spot for the planning sessions was Fort Lauderdale, Florida, then at the height of its chic. Carson and a group of writers and producers from the *Who Do You Trust?* staff would head down there and, in the words of Herb Sargent, who was to become head writer on *The Tonight Show,* "We'd sit around talking ideas all day, and get drunk at night." The pressure was on, and it was a scared crew down in Fort Liquordale.

The week before the new show was to air, the *New York World Telegram*'s TV writer described the intensity of the situation: "Next Monday, Johnny Carson steps onto an NBC stage to begin hosting one of the highest-rated shows on television. *The Tonight Show Starring Johnny Carson* has been eagerly anticipated for months, and thousands of words have been written about it in magazines and newspapers.

"One of the big questions everybody's been asking is 'What kind of a show is it going to be?' 'What kind of show is Johnny putting together?' To date, Johnny's answer, with a grin, has been 'Let's both wait and see.'

"Part of the story behind Monday night's debut lies in the preparation Carson has had for the show professionally and personally. Even though he's had over ten years broadcasting and telecasting experience, he's fashioned impromptu 'classrooms' out of his office and home with intent to broaden his knowledge about guests scheduled for the show. He keeps up to date by reading every book, newspaper, and magazine he can, for he knows the subjects covered in the show's unpredictable conversations demand a worldly-wise attitude . . . ."

All Johnny really had were his instincts and the Fort Lauderdale-born ideas of what the show should be. In aspects, Johnny's show would harken back to the earlier versions of *The Tonight Show,* and also to *Who Do You Trust?*. Gone were the hand-wringing, tears, and the political controversy of the Paar years. What was there was the best of the old formats and, of course, Carson's native comic capability and skill.

Art Stark, who had been the producer of *Who Do You Trust?* and the man responsible for its format, was hired by NBC to produce the new *Tonight Show* for Carson, and a lot of the *Trust* writers were brought along as well. But the new task was considerably more complicated than the old.

The Tonight Show in those days ran from 11:15 p.m. until 1:00 a.m. five days a week. This was the equivalent of doing three weeks of *Who Do You Trust?* shows every week. The task was draining.

103

The format settled upon for the new show called for: a fifteen-minute monologue followed by guests from the entertainment world (a regular *Tonight Show* feature); sketches and skits (something borrowed from the Allen format); stunts in which Johnny would participate (an idea borrowed from *Who Do You Trust?*); guests who were eccentric or offbeat but not well known (also borrowed from *Who Do You Trust?*); adventures into the audience (also from the old *Tonight Show*); and guests with books or ideas to discuss (from the *Today Show* version of *The Tonight Show*); and musical acts (a segment borrowed from all versions of *The Tonight Show* and designed to give the host at least a short breathing spell during the 105-minute show).

The new *Tonight Show* debuted on October 1, 1962. The guests were an eclectic set: Rudy Vallee, Joan Crawford, and Mel Brooks. Carson had spent hours viewing old Crawford movies and boning up on Vallee's history in preparation for the show.

"We wanted to get away from that old Paar idea that all the guests were just a gang of personal friends sitting around a living room. They weren't, and we weren't going to go along with that fiction," recalled a writer of those days. "We wanted to do something new."

The new *Tonight Show* scored a remarkably high forty share in the ratings and, despite some unevenness, continued to do well. Almost immediately what made the show a huge hit was Carson's opening monologue, combined with his winsome way with offbeat guests, and his ability to be a good sport.

A month after his premier performance, Johnny was interviewed by the *New York Times*. In the interview Carson spoke of his new daily schedule—a routine that has dominated his life for more than a quarter of a century:

" 'It's just about what I figured it would be,' he said. 'The schedule is rough. But I'm starting to settle down a little. It's one of those strange shows where you're at work from the time you get up in the morning until you go to bed at night.'

" 'I get up between nine and ten in the morning,' he said. 'I don't believe in jumping out of bed and shouting "Hey, hey, another day." I just grumble and sulk for a while. I don't really start to function until noon or afterwards.'

"From his Manhattan apartment, he usually travels to the studio at about two o'clock. At that time he tries to have read several newspapers that might provide ideas for topical remarks on the program.

" 'I don't try to avoid current events, and I don't consider politics taboo,' Mr. Carson said. 'No matter what area you take, you're going to be up for grabs as far as political comment is concerned. I believe that it's the kind of program where if you've got something to say about what's going on in this nutty world of ours, you should do it.'

"He spreads his political quips to cover both sides of the major parties. After Richard M. Nixon was defeated in his attempt to win the governorship of California, Mr. Carson said: 'But he's not giving up; now he's going to run for head of his family.'

"Soon afterward he said of Edward M. Kennedy, the youthful United States Senator-elect from Massachusetts and brother of President Kennedy: 'He was the only candidate who made his acceptance speech while wearing Dr. Dentons.'

"Mr. Carson is aware of occasional objections by viewers to what they consider offensive humor on the show. Not long ago one of his guests was . . . a young woman of some carriage, who conducts her own television program of setting-up exercises. On the Carson show, he joined her in doing some calisthenics. As

105

they stretched out on separate mats on the studio floor, he said to her, 'Would you like to leave a call?'

"The remark was criticized by a columnist for an afternoon newspaper. Mr. Carson, however, contended that under the circumstances, what he said was harmless.

" 'It depends on how you handle it,' he said. 'A smirk or a leer can make anything offensive. And, after all, we're on the air late at night when you would assume that children would be asleep. If you can't do something provocative now and then, the show would be pretty dull.'

"Although Mr. Carson believes that the star of such a program develops a personal rapport with the audience, he does not think his viewers are interested in his problems. 'I'm getting well paid for what I do,' he said. 'As President Truman once said, "If the heat's too much in the kitchen, get out." If the program became a personal burden for me, I'd get out.'

"He finds *The Tonight Show* different from anything he has tried before. 'It's a chess game,' he said, 'it changes right on the air. That's what makes it exciting.' "

But Carson's franchise in 1962 was far from secure. *The Tonight Show* then still belonged to NBC, not to Johnny Carson.

The show took off, though, and recognition of the new host's talents began to surface. For example, on November 14, 1962, something happened for the first time, something that's been repeated many times since. A joke—a political joke—from the monologue was reprinted in a gossip column.

It happened in Bob Williams' "On the Air" column in the *New York Post* when Williams led his column with the following:

"Johnny Carson on *Tonight* may have been the first comedian to chance a Nixon 'joke' since the former vice-president's bitter farewell address to reporters [following his loss to Governor

Edmund Brown in the California gubernatorial election]. Carson said that Nixon, since election day, had been working around his Beverly Hills home, had put in a new driveway, had shingled the roof and 'bricked up his mouth' . . . . It drew a seemingly hesitant studio laugh . . . ."

7

From Employee to Midnight Idol

I n the mid-sixties, *The Tonight Show* began at 11:15 p.m. (not at 11:30 Eastern time as it does now) and the first fifteen minutes were, of course, devoted to Johnny's monologue. And while the monologue was the most popular and most quoted portion of the new program, it was also, in the network's sometimes foggy eyes, the most dispensable portion of the program. During the 1964 political conventions, the monologue was often pre-empted by continuing reports from NBC's celebrated news team of Huntley and Brinkley. Johnny jokingly began to suggest to viewers that Huntley and Brinkley were, in fact, a new comedy team hired to open *The Tonight Show*. This, to the serious lads in the news department, seemed flip and undignified. Soon there were rumors that Johnny's contract would be bought out and that he'd be replaced by someone who had a proper attitude of respect for the news department. Of course, if the network looked closely, they'd find it was Johnny's political jokes which were being quoted in the papers and coffee shops around the country, not Huntley's or Brinkley's sonorous sentences about LBJ and Barry Goldwater. But network business success means little to newsmen. Johnny was the new boy on the block, and he was expected to behave with awe and respect towards the policies of the giant network and its news department.

Such policies had their origins, however, in less than dignified concerns. The very fact that *The Tonight Show* started at the awkward moment of 11:15 and not 11:30 was rooted, ironically enough, in the network's refusal to give the news department in New York and at local stations, another fifteen minutes of air time each night. And that policy in turn had originated with an advertiser's whim.

The Ruppert Brewing Company in New York, which had sponsored the original *Tonight Show*, liked having the show start at 11:15, and inertia had kept anyone from changing the show time—long after Ruppert Beer had burped out of the advertising picture.

But when local stations began to take the 11:15 to 11:30 spot for their own use, with expanded news shows and local advertising, the network did nothing to change its own scheduling to allow Carson's entire show to be seen nationally. Thus, for awhile, *The Tonight Show* was seen throughout much of the country without Carson's opening monologue—the local stations simply cut it out.

Failing to gain any support from the network in his insistence that the local stations should be required to carry the entire program, Johnny himself began to boycott the opening fifteen minutes of his own show. He knew, even if the network and the local station managers didn't, that the monologue was the best part of the program, so he simply decided to begin the monologue at 11:30.

During the first fifteen minutes, Ed McMahon, in a step which certainly assured his tenure on the show, filled in, chatting for fifteen minutes with the audience about the guests scheduled for the show. So, for a period of months, New York viewers saw *The Tonight Show* opened by Ed McMahon, who was then followed at 11:30 by Carson and his monologue.

NBC wasn't happy about having the star skip the opening of the show, and a large, noisy squabble between Carson and the NBC brass played itself out for months, until all parties hit upon a brilliant new solution: they would start the show at 11:30 and let it run for ninety minutes instead of 105.

This arrangement allowed all local newscasts to run for thirty minutes instead of fifteen, which made the local stations very happy. By the mid-sixties, local news broadcasting had changed from being an onerous public service into highly profitable programming.

Viewers and Carson were happier too, even though for Carson the monologue often caused trouble. Johnny's remarks were regularly misconstrued by special interest groups and blue noses. The famous gesture Carson now employs—a wave of the hand, a grimace, accompanied by the words "Now, don't write in now . . ."—dates from these days, when funny remarks resulted in bags of mail and hours of meetings dealing with frightened executives who were catching flak.

Some of the controversial episodes now seem merely strange.

One night, for example, it wasn't even Johnny's fault. Actor Ray Milland appeared on the show and for some reason began reciting a story about an afternoon swim he once took in a pool where the warmth of the water caused a momentary incontinence. A commissioner of the Federal Communications Commission, the agency which licenses television stations, lathered about the remark. Said Commissioner Robert E. Lee, "I feel the incident was pretty close to the line of indecency."

Johnny responded the next night by introducing the show with "Welcome to tonight's rendezvous in the bedroom. I'm Johnny Carson. I say that because the FCC has been mixing me up lately with Lenny Bruce." There were calls for Johnny's dismissal, and at one point, the network, allegedly aided by a then trusted Carson aide, was considering replacing Carson with someone like the innocuous Mike Douglas.

The show by the mid-sixties was earning more money for the network than any other show on television. In 1967, NBC was grossing more than $20 million annually from advertising on *The Tonight Show*. The bosses knew they had something, but they weren't entirely willing to trust their new host: after all, he was just an employee. What Carson knew, after the endless hassles over the monologue, was that he had to move beyond the status of house host and into a position of real power.

Hassles aside, there were many aspects of the show that Carson enjoyed. He especially liked discovering talent: Woody Allen, for example, first appeared on *The Tonight Show* in 1965; George Carlin in 1966; Richard Pryor in 1968; and David Brenner in 1971.

Bookers on *The Tonight Show* not only auditioned the hundreds of new performers who were regularly pitched to them by eager agents, managers, and family members, but also searched for new acts to make the show fresh and vital. And

Carson himself had a good eye for talent, frequently booking comics and performers he had seen on his jaunts around town. In 1965, a manic young female comic of no great looks and slightly beatnik mien caught his eye, and he booked her on the show. When she sat down in the guest chair after finishing her hilarious spiel, he said to her quietly, "You're very funny. You're going to make it." The young woman was startled because she had been on the verge of quitting show business entirely. Indeed, she had auditioned for *The Tonight Show* and had been rejected five times by Carson's talent bookers. She was Joan Rivers.

Carson also liked his comic characters, skits, and stunts, which saw him flying planes, skydiving, wrestling and throwing tomahawks. The tomahawk stunt was so popular that a tape of it is regularly replayed on the show's anniversary.

Singer Ed Ames, who was proud of his American Indian heritage, was invited to demonstrate the art of his ancestors by throwing axes at a cardboard model of a human. As luck would have it, one ax hit squarely into the cardboard man's crotch. Johnny's take—a long, shocked look into the camera—caused the audience to go wild, and made the event a classic of comedy.

But even though Carson was having fun, and making fun for others, his treatment at the hands of NBC remained shoddy, and resentments built.

Staffers said they could tell he was upset when he ordered a vodka and tonic (or, on truly bad days, a scotch and water) placed in the ever-present ceramic coffee mug on his desk. And they also agree he had much to be upset about.

His nominal pay was terrific (about $15,000 a week in 1967), but out of that amount he had to pay salaries not only to his personal staff but also to a number of *The Tonight Show* staffers.

And his offices and dressing room were shabby and

demeaning. "Just a little bigger than closets," recalls a former secretary, "and whenever Johnny would ask the network for improvements in the office space, he'd get nothing, just a huge amount of red tape, and a sneer."

Today, of course, Johnny Carson is a national figure, and no one remembers the names of those sneering network executives. But Carson's stardom did not come without the opposition of others. The thought of sudden cancellation in those early days saw Johnny hedge his bets by once again embarking on a career as a nightclub performer, something he once thought he had abandoned in the rough days following the collapse of his CBS show.

During the sixties, in addition to playing Las Vegas, he toured the country appearing at arenas, auditoriums, and fairs. His nightclub act was a bluer variation on his monologue and opening skits. Audiences loved it. The shows also built his confidence, allowing him to realize that his success came from his talent and experience, not from formats arranged by producers or programming notions offered by the network. The success of his tours convinced him once and for all that he was a star, not just a hired voice. But there would be serious confrontations, in which he would risk his career, before NBC would recognize Johnny's importance.

The first of these tests came when the American Federation of Television and Radio Artists (AFTRA)—which represented all on-air performers, including Carson—called a strike on March 28, 1967. Though the issues under discussion related primarily to news readers and disc jockeys, all of the union's members were ordered to walk.

Johnny left New York, flying to Fort Lauderdale with friends and business colleagues. While waiting for the strike to end,

Carson was startled to see NBC rebroadcast old *Tonight Show* tapes to fill his time slot. Furthermore, they were tapes from the 1966 Christmas season.

Carson sent a message to the network. He called the replay of the Christmasy shows during the springtime "ludicrous." And, to add injury to insult, the network would not compensate Carson for the reruns. Carson told them to cut it out. When NBC refused to stop the rebroadcasts, Carson—with some forethought—took his case to the press. The war of Johnny's independence was on.

"What is the price that should be paid for a rerun when it's used while your union is on strike?" Carson said to the press. Nothing, said the network. Quickly, Carson sent a letter to NBC, cancelling his contract.

Over the next month, the two bickered back and forth. NBC contended that the real question was money, and only money. NBC said Carson, then making about $720,000 a year, was holding them up for $1 million a year. Then the network suggested Carson wanted control of the show and that it wouldn't give that up.

Jack Paar went so far as to suggest that Carson was indeed just maneuvering for power and that the dispute over the rebroadcast tapes was just a ploy that would backfire with the public. Well-meaning friends cautioned Johnny to give up the dangerous game of negotiation and go back meekly to the network that provided him with a dressing room the size of a cell in a Civil War prison camp.

Anticipating that *The Tonight Show* would soon be a casualty of the war, other networks hurriedly moved to get late-night talk shows of their own ready.

Of course, there was more motivating Carson than the issue of the rerun tapes. Johnny *did* want a new contract, one that would free him from some of the network's interference, and give him more control of the show itself. Carson knew this was the right time to make a stand in order to make the show his own.

"*The Tonight Show* was not only a huge success and huge moneymaker for NBC," recalls an old-timer, "it was also an NBC institution. And NBC executives thought it was they, not Carson, who made the show work. They liked to believe the show did not depend on Carson for its success.

"The brass and a few of the NBC producers, including Art Stark, who had been with Johnny since the *Who do You Trust?* years, felt that Johnny was just a replaceable part of the show. They thought they could get just anyone in there to host the show and it would be a hit."

During the strike, NBC in fact did call in other prospective hosts, including Bob Newhart and singer Jimmy Dean, and began to prep them to succeed Carson. But they also did try in good faith to negotiate a new contract with Carson.

The AFTRA strike ended, and Carson was expected to go back to work. But he remained unhappy with the terms of the new contract being offered him, and stayed down in Florida. The night he was expected back on the show, Jimmy Dean, not Carson, sat in the host's chair, and next to Dean was, of all people, Ed McMahon.

Ed had decided to go back to work, risking Johnny's wrath rather than the network's. After all, he had mortgage payments. But during the show with Dean, Ed looked exceedingly uncomfortable—maybe because of Dean's barnyard jokes.

While Dean's shows were a disaster, ABC proceeded with plans for its own late-night talk show, to star Las Vegas comedian Joey Bishop. NBC had no suitable replacement for Carson, and competition was building. NBC, taking stock of the situation, came back to the bargaining table and with Carson's lawyer, Arnold Grant, agreed to a new contract.

Johnny had triumphed. Under the new contract, he was given complete control of the show, including the power to hire and fire personnel (previously, that had been the network's affair), and money to pay a staff. He was also given a hefty increase in pay to $1 million a year. The three-year contract also forbade either side from discussing its terms. But each side was allowed an announcement.

Johnny said: "I'm grateful to the many, many people who have been kind enough to say they missed me. Television makes friendship possible with a host of unknown persons. I hope to repay their generosity with the very best that is in me."

An NBC spokesman said: "We are delighted at Johnny's return, and we know the feeling is shared by millions of viewers throughout the country who enjoy his unique brand of humor and intimate warmth."

Thus, the network was vanquished, and Johnny emerged as a superpower who could fully control his show. All that remained was to take care of some other housekeeping matters. Pundits predicted that Ed McMahon, for showing up to work with Dean, would be the first to go. They were wrong.

Carson had always liked McMahon, and while they did not socialize as much as they had in the very early years, Johnny recognized the value of Ed on the show. He also sympathized with the tough position Ed had been in when he decided to return to work at the end of the strike. Ed would stay. But others who had failed to recognize what Johnny did and how well he did it, would be out.

The afternoon preceding Johnny's first post-strike *Tonight*

Show, Johnny asked the show's producer, Art Stark, to visit him at his East Side Manhattan apartment.

Stark, who was an employee of NBC, had been at *The Tonight Show* as long as Johnny. Indeed, the two had worked together for ten years. Stark had been the producer and presiding genius behind *Who Do You Trust?* He had come up with the idea of down-playing the quiz part of the show, in order to concentrate on the verbal by-play between the host and his eccentric guests. And Stark believed that he was responsible for Johnny Carson's success as the host.

Over the years the two had been close. It was Stark who had given the bride away at Johnny's second wedding. But Stark had grown increasingly difficult to work with. Frequently he vetoed ideas for the show and tried at times to overrule Johnny.

"The fact is," recalled a staffer, "Johnny had grown a lot over the years, in confidence and in skill. He was really running the show, and Art was growing more and more restrictive."

For months before the strike, Stark had been a problem, and staffers recall Johnny asking them, "What am I going to do about Art?" Under the old contract, there was nothing Johnny could do. That decision was left to NBC, which believed in the rule of producers, not stars. But under the new contract, the decision was Johnny's. So before the first post-strike show, Carson called Art. He'd have the grace to give him the word in person, and alone.

Stark recalled the meeting this way: "I walked in thinking it was a routine matter pertaining to a forthcoming show.

" 'Art,' Johnny said, 'I want another producer, not associated with NBC, on the show.'

"When do you want me to leave?

" 'Right now.' "

(A staffer, Rudy Tellez, replaced Stark until 1970, when Freddie de Cordova took the job; seventeen years later he is still *The Tonight Show* producer.)

Carson's treatment of Stark was regarded by some as harsh and disloyal. But it must be remembered that the show really had become Carson's—he was the one who made it work. Some of the old-timers resented Johnny's coming into his own, while others suggest that Stark was dragging the show down with his vetoes and hidebound ways. "Johnny doesn't like people who don't pull their weight," said Ed McMahon, who also knows that Johnny can be tremendously loyal to people who do pull their weight. The new contract of 1967 and the firing of Art Stark meant that Johnny was now solely responsible for the success or failure of *The Tonight Show*. It also meant a better dressing room.

Johnny's successful battles with NBC, his new contract, and his triumphant return made the media realize he was more than a TV host. He was a major American entertainer. When Johnny returned to the air in May 1967, he made the cover of *Time* magazine which billed him as the first "midnight idol." And for the first time, the press tried to analyze his popularity. *Time* defined a *Tonight Show* audience that was far different from the one Art Stark thought was watching.

"His viewers," *Time* reported, "are mostly urban and at least high school educated, young enough to stay up late with ease, or successful enough not to have to show up too early for work. Jimmy Stewart watches, so do Bobby Kennedy, Ed Sullivan, Nebraska Governor Norbert Tiemann, Robert Merrill, and Nelson Rockefeller.

"Thanks to his popularity, the network is dominant in the late-night time slot . . . . CBS, whose affiliates generally run movies opposite Carson, tried to buy him away from NBC but as Johnny put it, 'I would feel as out of place on another network as Lurleen Wallace giving a half-time pep talk to the Harlem Globe Trotters.' "

He was now in the big time. But the night he returned to the air, ABC aired its new late-night talk show with Joey Bishop. And his first guest? None other than Jack Paar. It's a jungle in television land.

During this period, from Johnny's arrival in Hollywood in the early fifties to his takeover of *The Tonight Show,* Johnny led—as he leads today—a very private life, with few close friends, with still fewer who are willing to say anything about their very powerful friend. One of them, however, gives a unique insight into the life of a star in the making. Jack Narz, a highly successful announcer and game-show host, who now lives in Beverly Hills, recalls:

"We met when Johnny first came out to Los Angeles in the early fifties. He was doing *Carson's Cellar* downstairs in a studio, and I was upstairs where I was one of the announcers for *Queen for a Day.* He used to run up and stick his head in the door once in a while, that's how we met.

"Later on in Los Angeles, we became neighbors; we lived about a half mile from each other. Our kids went to the same school.

"We both probably felt the same way about the business. We were both happy go lucky. We felt lucky we were working and did anything that came along. I wouldn't say he was overly ambitious. He could have been inside, though, deep within himself.

"Back in Encino, we had lots of friends in common. Mostly the parents at the school where his kids and mine went. It was called Egremont French Day School, and both Jody and my wife were members of the Mothers Club. And the husbands, we'd call ourselves the 'Mother Grabbers.' When the Mothers Club had their meetings, the Mother Grabbers would play poker and go to different guys' houses.

"John didn't have a pool at that time, so his kids used to spend a lot of time at our house swimming. We'd go to each other's house for barbecues and things. We continued that when we both later were living outside of New York City in Westchester County.

"I remember the first letter we got from the Carsons after they moved to New York in the mid-fifties. I looked at the postmark and said, 'I've never heard of this town: MAMA-RO-NECK.' It was Mamaroneck. Well, within a matter of months, I myself was in New York doing a quiz-show called *Dotto*, and I rented a house in the next town to them in Larchmont, and we later found a house in Mamaroneck. This was before they moved to Harrison. We went looking at houses together.

"He and Jody weren't getting along, and when he had an offer to do a Broadway play, he took an apartment in Manhattan, which was what he wanted to do anyway. We still went out to dinner together, honking around, and hitting the bars and things.

"I was doing *Dotto* at the time. That's the show that caused the quiz show scandals. The whole world came crashing down around my ears. Ours was the first show to get into trouble. That lit the fuse, then the bomb started going off all over town.

"John and I would go to work together. He had a little motorboat that he kept on the river in Manhattan, and we would go home in his boat up to New Rochelle where he docked it. Then one of our wives would pick us up. We spent quite a bit of time together.

"We used to play golf together up at the Westchester Country Club. We used to play with Jan Murray and Hal March. John looked at golf as 'a nice way to screw up a walk in the country.' He wasn't thrilled with the game.

"A few years later, around 1961, when I was hosting *The Price Is Right* and putting *Video Village* on the air, we played poker practically every night at John's place with Ed McMahon and Bill Nimo, and a navy chaplain named Father Wadowitz. We had a little rat pack of our own going. John had a little apartment on York Avenue, and he was still doing *Who Do You Trust?* He and Jody were separated.

"In 1962, just about the time he was being talked about to take over *The Tonight Show,* I had an offer to come back to California and do a show called *Seven Keys.* It was an opportunity for me to get back to California, which I wanted to do in the worst way. I wasn't too crazy about New York.

"Johnny and I at the time had the same managers—Shields and Bruno—and shortly after Johnny got *The Tonight Show,* Tom Shields called me in Salt Lake City where I was doing something. John was in Phoenix or someplace like that doing a benefit for the B'nai B'rith or something. Tom called and said, 'How about the three of us—you, John and myself—meeting in Las Vegas over the weekend?'

"Tom said, 'John is real nervous and scared to death because he's going to do *The Tonight Show,* and he'd like some company for the weekend.' So we all went to Vegas and held Johnny's hand. He was a nervous wreck. While we were there, we went to Sammy Davis's show, and that's where Sammy announced to his audience that John was about to take over *The Tonight Show.* John stood up and took a bow.

"Then John went back to New York and did *The Tonight Show.* We didn't see much of each other for a while. The first time I saw him after that was the first time they did a series of *Tonight*

Shows from L.A. He still wasn't a New Yorker. He was still a kind of Nebraska-type guy.

"What I'm trying to say is when they brought the show out here [to California] they weren't treated the way they are today. They put cast and crew up at one hotel, the same hotel. John called me up and said, 'I don't want to stay with all those guys. Can you get me a room reservation somewhere else and a rental car?' I said sure. So I made a reservation at the Beverly Hills Hotel with a car and got him a blind date, and we went out to dinner.

"On his first trip to Vegas, to perform at the stage show at the Sahara, I went up to see him, and we spent some time together. After the show, we'd go into the lounge and heckle Don Rickles when he was doing a lounge act. But that's basically it.

"When I first met John, he was sort of a shy and reticent guy. I think he still is a little bit. I can remember one incident. He was having some dental work done, and it required filing his teeth down, and he didn't want to be seen in public, so I think I was the only person he ever saw or ever visited for the days, or the week, or however long it took for the work to be done. He'd come to my house, and we'd sit around and shoot the bull, and he wouldn't worry about smiling and me seeing those funny little stubs there. They gave him caps for the teeth. He didn't want anyone else to see him.

"That's about as close as we were. We weren't together day and night. We didn't do everything together.

"After he took over *The Tonight Show* I didn't see too much of him, except for that time when they first came out here. I was here all the time, not in New York.

"One time, I went back to New York to help out on a show when a friend—the host—died.

"Johnny had married Joanne by then, and they had moved somewhere near the U.N.. So I called NBC and got his secretary. I gave her my number where I'd be staying. I didn't hear from him.

"Then on one of my trips within a couple of months of that, I was in New York at the airport, JFK, catching a flight to L.A., and Joanne was there to meet Johnny who was flying in from Vegas.

"And Joanne and I had a brief conversation. She said, 'Omigod, Johnny would love to hear from you. Why don't you give him a call?' So I called again and got his secretary, and again he didn't call back.

"So we just drifted apart from then on. I saw him at the Emmy Awards two years ago out at the Pasadena Civic. He was talking to Dennis James. I don't think he recognized me at first. Dennis said, 'Well, you know Jack Narz, don't you?'

"And John said, 'Omigod,' and threw his arms around me and kissed me on the cheek and asked me if I was still living in the desert. I said, 'Johnny, that was twenty years ago.'

"There was no rift between us; we just drifted apart. It certainly wasn't anything that I did or anything that John did. We just sort of went our separate ways."

8
Tiny Tim
and the
Competition

G uests on *The Tonight Show* often speak about being caught unaware by Johnny, of being asked about matters they hadn't planned to discuss. That's Johnny's way of keeping the show electric and alive. "The show is what we create as we go along," he once said. The idea, of course, is to provide interesting television. Mariette Hartley, now the anchor of the *CBS Morning Show,* says the experience can be "sexy and exciting." Suzanne Pleshette has described Johnny's technique as "thrilling." But these two know how to talk, and they enjoy ad-libbing. For most guests, however, the show is jarring, but that's part of what makes it interesting: the eliciting of the offbeat, the dramatic, the apt-to-be-talked-about.

Nowadays, Carson has become an institution, and the excitement and appeal that he generates through his interviews keeps audiences watching. But in the late sixties and early seventies, when copycat talk shows were all over television, *The Tonight Show* resorted to some strange means to stay in the public eye.

In December 1969, Carson's staff engineered a bizarre stunt that resulted in the highest ratings *The Tonight Show* has ever received.

It was the on-air wedding of singer Tiny Tim and his fiancée, one Miss Vicki. Tiny Tim, a long-haired giant of a man, was a true show-biz freak of the late sixties. He looked like a flower child who had been fed on steroids, though his songs were schmaltzy, Tin-pan Alley tunes, like his version of "Tiptoe through the Tulips."

Tiny, who had been spied roaming around Times Square (where to this day still he roams, *sans* wife, hair down to his shoulders, clothes not so natty, but still very much the celebrity, nodding hellos to the few who still recognize him), had been invited on *The Tonight Show* earlier in the year, primarily for the shock value. Not only was he odd looking and odd sounding, he had odd habits, such as bathing an extraordinary number of times during each day. With Johnny as interlocutor, Tiny turned out to be a hilarious *Tonight Show* guest. Later, when talent coordinator Craig Tennis learned that Tiny was going to marry, Tennis booked the wedding on the show. The event, as anticipated, not only smothered the competition in the ratings, but also made the papers for days afterwards, as columnists and critics alike deplored what they saw as the trivialization of wedding vows by television, *The Tonight Show*, and Tiny Tim. But that was when the talk-show wars were going full blast and *The Tonight Show* was seeking to be sensational.

Until 1967, Johnny really had the talk-show franchise in America all to himself. But success, combined with the show's low cost and high profit, inspired copies. (Guests appeared for union scale of around $300, not for the huge fees variety shows had once been forced to pay.)

Every major supplier of programs to television stations—the Westinghouse 'Group W' operation, ABC, CBS, and others—quickly sought to cash in. By the early seventies, there were four major talk shows out of New York every day, and others were broadcasting from Philadelphia, Cleveland, and other cities. Among the hosts of the new, imitation *Tonight Shows* were Joey Bishop, Merv Griffin (both Bishop and Griffin had, in the Jack Paar days, served as substitute hosts on Paar's *Tonight Show*), Mike Douglas, David Frost, Virginia Graham, Phil Donahue, Dick Cavett, and others.

The Joey Bishop Show on ABC was the first of the shows to compete directly with *The Tonight Show* during the same air time. But from the start *The Joey Bishop Show* seemed doomed.

On its first night, April 17, 1967, Ronald Reagan, then governor of California and the opening show's special guest, was fifteen minutes late. On the second night, Buddy Greco, that night's big guest, was given a stunning introduction by Joey. But when the introduction was over, there was no Buddy. The camera stared at an empty stage. No one backstage had bothered to cue Greco and he, unaware that he was to go on, blithely sat in his dressing room, chatting privately with well-wishers. The Bishop show stumbled along for two years, until Joey, finally fed up, walked off. The show, hosted by substitutes, closed a month later.

ABC replaced it in December 1969 with a show hosted by Dick

Cavett. Cavett, who had worked as a writer for both Carson and Paar—and as a stand-up comic and talk-show guest—had recently been the host of a number of successful talk shows.

In March 1968, he had been given a five-day-a-week, ninety-minute, daytime talk show on ABC. This lasted until January 1969. From May 1969 to the early autumn of that year, he went on three times a week in prime time. Then in December 1969, he was given the former Bishop slot opposite *The Tonight Show.*

Cavett tried different approaches, including in-depth interviews with the likes of Woody Allen, Orson Welles, Charlton Heston, and Jack Lemmon, which were highly praised by the critics ("intelligent alternative programming" *Time* called it). Yet Cavett was never able to achieve good ratings, let alone loosen Carson's hammerlock on late night. Finally, in January 1973, ABC took Cavett's show off the air.

With the kick-off of Merv Griffin's show in August 1969, CBS was the last to enter the late-night ratings war. Griffin, who had originally been a game-show host, had hosted daytime talk shows since 1962. With English character actor Arthur (The Butler) Treacher as his sidekick, and a manner as silky as nylon, it was hoped Griffin would be a successful alternative, but Griffin, like Bishop and then Cavett, did not even come close to unseating Carson. On February 11, 1972, Merv Griffin's show was cancelled by CBS. Griffin, however, had the foresight and business sense to syndicate his show to independent stations, stations not affiliated with the networks. Griffin, who would become one of the richest men in America from his TV production enterprises like the game show *Wheel of Fortune,* continued to work on his show until 1986.

Although Johnny was fond of making fun of Griffin's oily delivery and his penchant for "theme shows" devoted to offbeat topics like swimming suits of the rich and trim, Carson and Griffin were friends. Indeed, Johnny's brother, Dick Carson, the former director of *The Tonight Show*, directed *The Merv Griffin Show* in its last dozen years. When Griffin closed the show in 1986 and sold his production company for hundreds of millions of dollars, he was invited to appear on *The Tonight Show* as a guest, which he did.

During the height of the late-night talk-show wars, from 1969 to 1972, there was one other entry of note, *The David Frost Show*, which, like the Carson and Griffin shows, originated in New York. Frost was a celebrated British television interviewer, famous for his thorough homework on his guests, and his odd crunched-up posture. He specialized in detailed interviews with a wide range of guests including Billy Graham, Timothy Leary, Richard Nixon, Henny Youngman, Elizabeth Taylor, and obscure British rock groups. These interviews often veered off into the almost absurd with questions like "What is your idea of love?" frequently popping up.

Frost's show was a syndicated, non-network broadcast, produced by the Westinghouse 'Group W' organization, which dropped it in 1972 when Merv Griffin's show became available to them.

The other talk-show hosts—Mike Douglas, John Davidson, Phil Donahue, Virginia Graham, and others—appeared primarily in the daytime, not the late-night hours.

Although Griffin, Bishop, Cavett, and Frost never threatened Johnny's ratings, the period from 1969 to 1972, when all were on, resulted in some major changes for *The Tonight Show* and for Johnny Carson.

Fred de Cordova, who had joined the show as a producer in 1970, grew concerned about the fact that three shows—*The*

Tonight Show, The Merv Griffin Show, and *The David Frost Show*—were all being produced out of New York, and that the same guests were starting to pop up on all three shows. Indeed, there were times when a guest would appear on the Griffin show and the Carson show within a matter of days, if not hours. As a way of putting new faces on the show, de Cordova and Carson decided to produce it out of Hollywood at least a few months of the year.

These sojurns in Los Angeles, complete with endless jokes about the Sheraton-Unbelievable Hotel in Burbank, where the staff camped, became ratings winners. Not only were audiences entranced by the new and slightly silly guests that Carson cajoled out of the Hollywood-work, they loved the new characters and skits inspired by the mad L.A. lifestyle.

It was in these jaunts that the Mighty Carson Art Players, so named in homage to Fred Allen's Los Angeles radio troupe, the Mighty Allen Art Players, came to the fore with such celebrated Carson characters as Art Fern and the Tea Time Matinee.

Fern, played by Carson, was the prototypical Los Angeles TV salesman. "Art Fern, the tea time movie host," says Carson, "grew out of a local slickster salesman on TV; he had a little pencil mustache and a very bad toupee, that looked like it had been painted on his head. It's just a takeoff on the guys out here in California who do their own selling, whether they're selling the 'miracle vegetable cutter,' or whatever."

Art Fern, whose commercials were accompanied by graphs of the L.A. freeway system ("and then you get to the Slauson Cutoff . . . stop, get out and cut off your slauson . . . and drive on until you reach the Fork in the Road!"), and the wonderful matinee lady. For years, the matinee lady, a buxom, dumber-than-thou assistant who always seemed to be caught in a lewd embrace with Art Fern as the cameras came back from whatever silly movie was on the Tea Time Matinee, was played by actress Carol Wayne. She was one of the highlights of Carson's early trips to Los Angeles and appeared frequently after the show moved permanently to Los Angeles. Unfortunately, she drowned during a Mexican vacation in January 1983 at the age of 39.

De Cordova, who, of course, had lived in Los Angeles during his years as a producer of movies (he produced Ronald Reagan's celebrated *Bedtime for Bonzo* and is now a great friend of the First Family), urged Carson to move the show entirely to Los Angeles. It was an idea that took some getting used to. After all, it was in Los Angeles in 1956 that Carson's career had foundered. His success had come entirely in New York.

Continued success in New York, however, would have meant seeking out the truly bizarre, like Tiny Tim's wedding, as fodder for the show. So, while the show with Tiny Tim's wedding was a huge hit, it was also the beginning of the end of the New York *Tonight Show.*

Something else was also starting to end. Marriage number two was on the rocks in the early seventies.

9

'This Guy
Can Kill You.'

I n the early seventies, *The Tonight Show* had not yet become the national institution it is nowadays. Then it was as awkward as an adolescent, sometimes serving as the silly, but popular, arena for side-show events like the wedding of Tiny Tim, and then, on almost the next night, serving as a forum for public figures like Hubert Humphrey. The show was immensely popular and well liked but it hadn't yet found the voice and tone it now has.

During this period as Johnny was becoming a superstar, a man who could influence public opinion on national issues, he was subject to major conflicts about what *The Tonight Show* should be. And these problems added to severe pressures in his personal life, which would result in his separation from Joanne in 1970 and their divorce in 1972.

Joanne said at the time, "I don't know what caused the split. For myself, I can't think of any reasons for it. There was no other reason than that Johnny wanted his freedom. When somebody you love wants his freedom, what can you say or do? I knew in my heart that I had worked 100 percent of my capacity. I'd given him everything I could and then some. It wasn't my fault. It wasn't his fault. It was just sad. When somebody says, 'I don't love you anymore,' you just can't fight it.

"I don't think anyone can ever mean as much to me. We had a perfect relationship. He was everything I'd ever wanted. You know when you're a little girl, you dream of finding the man on the white horse. Well, I found him in Johnny."

The press reported a difficult and painful divorce. According to newspaper accounts, Joanne testified in tears that Johnny locked her out of their United Nations Plaza apartment in New York City. Yet today there seems to be no trace of vindictiveness in Joanne, who told us, "There were no real problems in the marriage. It's just that I couldn't live in the limelight is all—I was raised in a convent. Also, there was illness—I was hypoglycemic.

"Johnny was definitely understanding. He knew that kind of life was hard on me . . . that I was losing touch with my roots."

When their divorce was finally settled in the summer of 1972, she received $200,000 in a cash payment, art then worth $250,000, and annual alimony of $100,000. That's when the jokes about divorce started on *The Tonight Show*, which by that time had been fully and entirely moved to Los Angeles.

A more relaxed, outgoing Johnny soon settled into Hollywood. His humor, however, remained unchanged by the move west. On the air, he quoted a Wisconsin congressman, Harold V. Froelich, who for some reason seemed to think there was about to be a nationwide toilet paper shortage. There was no shortage, but Johnny mentioned the congressman's tissue issue on the air and instigated a national run on toilet paper that had supermarkets and tissue manufacturers working overtime for weeks.

In 1972, a political scandal would create the occasion for Johnny to emerge as a national spokesman—in the manner of Will Rogers. Johnny's wit would rise above being merely funny, it would be a satirical, but common-sensical, expression of a country's anger at politicians who had betrayed the nation's trust. The scandal, of course, was Watergate.

In the maelstrom of confusing opinion and commentary surrounding the early days of Watergate, the lengthy political scandal which began in 1972 with the discovery that the offices of the Democratic National Committee had been burglarized by a White House authorized "dirty tricks" squad and ended in 1974 with the forced resignation and pardon of President Richard M. Nixon, there was no clear sense of where the country stood on the issue. Columnists and pundits sympathetic to the administration argued that a silent majority in the nation backed the beleagured Nixon. Others insisted that an outraged republic wanted his immediate ouster. The true nature of public opinion, even when measured by pollsters, remained murky. Until one night when, in the course of his monologue, Johnny first joked about the eighteen-minute gap in Rosemary Wood's tapes, and the audience roared its approval. For months a stream of hilarious jokes about the White House and politicians followed. "When I heard Johnny Carson making fun of Nixon," recalls one politician, "I knew then that Nixon was finished. Carson was, as usual, right on top of the pulse of the American people. He was saying what they felt."

Carson himself later said of Watergate, Agnew, and Nixon: "I guess, like a lot of people, I felt let down. I resented people like Nixon and Agnew moralizing from the tops of their voices about morality and putting down the kids who didn't want to fight Vietnam . . . when they [Nixon, Agnew, etc.] were deceiving everybody. I think when you're in those kinds of jobs and you have the public trust, then you should play it by the book."

Shortly before Nixon's resignation, Carson told *TV Guide:* "In nightclubs and on television, I've been doing quite a bit of material on Watergate. And the audiences love it. But I don't *attack* the president. I just do jokes about what is going on in Washington—a situation I didn't create. What I'm doing, in effect, is saying a lot of things the audience would like to say but doesn't have the opportunity to say. On this show, I'm able to comment on what's happening every day, which is what people want to hear."

"This guy, Carson, can kill you," says a campaign advisor. "If he puts your man away with a few zingers and then keeps it up, there's no doubt it has an effect on people taking your guy as seriously as before."

Rick DuBrow, the television editor of the *Los Angeles Herald* put it this way, "Carson is not only the best comedian in the country today, and more consistently funny than NBC's other politician-needlers on *Saturday Night Live*, he also unnerves the politicos because of his unpredictability.

"Unlike Bob Hope, who invariably is on the side of the Establishment, Carson, a suit-and-tie Nebraskan who *looks* like the Establishment, has a real acerbic streak that the Establishment can't write off as coming from a far-out performer."

In 1982 the reluctantly retiring United States senator from California, S. I. Hayakawa, said Carson had caused him "real damage" by making jokes about his sleeping in public and said, "The people who get their basic political information from Johnny Carson remember nothing else about my career." Sleepy Sam, who first got into trouble when he fell asleep during classes held at Harvard for freshman congressional legislators, dropped his re-election campaign after polls showed him trailing other political hopefuls for the Republican nomination.

One of the monologues that Carson did shortly before the 1980 election, when hapless Jimmy Carter was running for re-election, was a virtual parade of political jokes:

"Let's talk about politics," Johnny said. "It's going to be an interesting year coming up. There's no doubt that Carter's going to run for president in 1980 because he's definitely decided to run for the vacancy in the White House.

"The Republicans have got some exciting candidates. There's Baker, Crane, Dole. How does one describe Bob Dole? In the parking lot of life, Dole is a Chrysler.

"I have nothing against Bob Dole. He is not the most exciting, charismatic personality around. He recently willed his body to science, and they contested the will.

"So far Ronald Reagan is the front-runner among the Republicans, and they keep trying to say that Ronnie is, you know, too old. I don't really think so. I mean, he's getting along but not—certainly not—well let me put it this way: most politicians quote Lincoln, but not many from personal conversations.

"I have a feeling I'm going to hear from Ron about that one."

And in the same 1979 monologue he turned his attention to the then raging oil crisis. "Standard Oil," he said, "was the last oil company to announce their third quarter profits. What do you think theirs were? They were only up 110 percent. Yeah, yeah. Exxon already announced they were 118. Mobil is 118, Texaco 98, Chevron about 156, and Sohio was something like 212. But the oil companies . . . Have you seen the full-page ads they are taking in the newspapers? They are saying they're not making all that money; it just looks that way.

"Boy, that's like Dolly Parton saying, 'Sure they're big, but they're not bigger than last year.' "

When in 1987 Arizona Governor Bruce Babbitt announced his presidential candidacy, Carson retorted, "With a name like that, he sounds like a friend of Elmer Fudd's, not a president."

While he was building a reputation as a national political pundit, he was also becoming a part of the Beverly Hills scene. At first, he seemed not to know how popular he was in the strange new community, and sometimes it wasn't easy to know when the friendliness of other stars was for real or not. Irving Fein, who was Jack Benny's manager, recalled one incident:

"Impersonators often called Johnny . . . [but] on Johnny's very first visit to the [West] Coast, Jack Benny called him at the Beverly Hills Hotel and told him, 'Listen, Johnny, if you need me, or if someone falls out on you at the last minute, call me, and I'll be happy to appear on your show.'

"Johnny was so certain that it was an impersonator, he coldly thanked him and hung up. Jack came into my office later that day and told me that he had called Carson, but Carson had been very unfriendly to him. I called Fred de Cordova, [producer of *The Tonight Show*] and asked if Johnny was angry with Jack for any reason, and I told him about the phone call. He spoke to Johnny about it, and Johnny, who had always liked Jack and admired him, promptly phoned and invited him to be on the show the next night, explaining about his mistaken impression."

Johnny's relationship with Jack Benny went back years—even further than many people thought. Johnny's first major network appearance on TV in 1952, when he was just a local comic, was on the Benny show. Fein remembers it this way: "The writers came up with a funny routine for Carson. He told the star that he was Johnny's idol and had been his idol for the two years that he, Johnny, had been in the business. When Jack beamed with delight at the praise, Johnny asked him if he'd mind if he, Johnny, made a few suggestions. He then proceeded to tell Jack that he spoke too slowly, that he stared at the audience too long, that he shouldn't put his hand on his cheek so often . . . . And all the while Jack kept interrupting to ask him how long he had been in show business."

When Benny donated his own memorabilia to the library at the University of California at Los Angeles (UCLA), Carson contributed an amazing reminiscence, duly recorded by Irving Fein:

"When I was a student at the University of Nebraska, Jack had a tremendous influence on me—on my understanding of comedy construction and timing. I still have a whole tape I did in college in 1948. Jack never got to hear it. I wish he had—but I told him about it. It was a thesis I did on radio comedy.

"I was twenty-one at the time. What I did was to tape all the big comedy shows: Jack's show . . . Fred Allen . . . Bob Hope . . . Fibber McGee and Molly . . . Herb Shriner, everything that was on. Then I took excerpts from those programs to illustrate how jokes were constructed. The running gags, the toppers, the whole development of humor.

"Many people say some of my mannerisms are like Jack's. Well, I think *all* comedians have 'ears'. They pick up, mimic, and eventually fall into certain patterns. I realize now that, in the early days of my career, I *was* too much like Jack. I tried to emulate him, which was wrong. But I *idolized* Jack. He had more influence on me than, say, Bob Hope, who is a joke-teller, a one liner. Fred Allen had some influence on me, too. I enjoyed his wit, his construction of lines, his word pictures. But without question, Jack and his show were the most tremendous influences on my development, on what I tried to do, on what I've become.

"Like so many of my generation, I grew up listening to Jack on radio. I was a completely devoted Benny fan for as far back as I can remember.

"I was seventeen years old the first time I saw Jack. I hitchhiked to California and went to see one of his radio show tapings at CBS. I was fresh out of high school, and about to go into the service. But first, I wanted to see Hollywood and Jack.

"I can never forget what a thrill it was actually being in his audience. Frank Fontaine was his guest doing the character of J. L. C. Sivoney, the sweepstakes winner. He subsequently appeared many times on Jackie Gleason's program as the drunk.

"Eight years later, in 1951, I had my first picture taken with Jack over at CBS. I had gone to a taping of his at the studio on Sunset and Gower. At that point, I had left the Midwest, come out here, and was doing a radio show, *Carson's Corner,* on the local CBS station, KNX. I was on every morning for *five minutes*, from 8:55 to 9:00 a.m. Jack was very generous, posing with me for that publicity photo. I'm sure he had no idea who I was.

"Later, I did a program called the *Sunday Show.* One week when Fred Allen came out from New York to be on with me, Jack visited the studio. That was the first time I actually *met* him.

"Many stories have been written about Jack's influence on me. They are all true. I can show you things I did in the early days, in which I was so close to his style, it embarrasses me now. But every comedian, when he's going through a formative period, takes a lot from everybody, for awhile. All the comics I've talked to admit it.

"When I discussed this with Jack, he told me that as a young man in vaudeville, he was influenced by Frank Fay. And I know Jackie Gleason picked up a little from Oliver Hardy.

"Most of all, from the standpoint of timing and structure, Jack was the key influence on me. Basically, I, like him, am a reaction comedian. I play off of the things that are happening around me. That is what works for me on *The Tonight Show*. When things happen around me, I can play off them by reaction, timing, pauses, and looks.

"Over the years, I learned another very important thing from Jack. If *other* people on your show are good, it makes *you* better. The stronger the other performers are, the greater it is for the whole program. I not only learned that—I've gained from it. On my show, the funnier and stronger Ed McMahon, Doc Severinsen, and Tommy Newsom are, the better it is for me and the entire show.

"No matter how funny Rochester, Phil Harris, Don Wilson, Dennis Day, or Mary were, it was always *The Jack Benny Show* people talked about and critics wrote about.

"When Jack had guest stars, he stood back, gave them the best material, and never was bothered when they got most of the laughs. He realized instinctively that it only strengthened him. But, in truth, there are very few comics who could have stood it. Most of them want and *need* all the funny lines for themselves.

"Most comedians are, by nature, very mercurial, especially in their anger, but not Jack. I never saw him display any temperament. He was the most disciplined performer I ever met.

"Overall, Jack seemed to be a very secure man. I know of

only one area in which he had insecurities. We talked about it on several occasions. Jack felt he was not sufficiently well read. He regretted his lack of a formal education. One time, at my house, I started discussing something, and I recall Jack saying, 'I really don't know about those things . . .'

"I felt strange, being so much younger than he was. But he was being very honest. I heard that one of the few personal appearances he ever turned down was an invitation to address the student body at Harvard. He said he felt he just couldn't face all those university students.

"Still, he not only overcame a great deal of this, he made it work for him. His language was grammatically correct, but because of his own lack of a formal education, he never talked down to his audiences, or used words that would have needed explanation.

"I think the reason Jack was able to sustain his career for so long is quite simple. *People like him.* If an audience likes a performer, he can get away with anything. If they don't like you, it doesn't make any difference how clever or witty you are . . . It just won't work!

"Performers like Jack, who sustain over the years, are the ones people identify with—as a person as well as an entertainer. I have seen a lot of clever performers come and go simply because the audience just didn't like them, didn't care about them. Jack's audiences always cared.

"Jack never acted like he had a superior quality, that's why everyone could identify with him. It may sound dull to keep praising him, to make him sound so saintlike. People always look for *something* in a life like Jack's. Something to add pizzazz. But with Jack, what it comes down to is *the man was what he was.*

"One night, a few of us were sitting around, just talking. Sinatra was there, George Burns, a few others. We were discussing some mundane thing, like how to prepare a decent cup of coffee. Suddenly, Jack began to laugh. 'People think we lead such exotic, glamorous lives. They imagine the parties we go to are all wild orgies, and here we are talking about a cup of coffee. Wouldn't they be disappointed if they could hear our conversation!'

"Jack didn't have the jealousy you often find in the entertainment world, which is very much a big ego business, especially in the comedy field. Many comedians don't even like to go and see other comics because they would have to hear them get big laughs! Jack was the other way around. He was the best audience in the world. If he saw somebody he liked, he'd call me and say, 'Gee, I saw this great kid. Why don't you put him on your show?' Invariably, I did . . . .

"Jack was so secure about his talent, perhaps because down deep he knew nobody could do what he could . . . . Really, no one could steal from Jack. You had to be Jack to do what he did. It was his attitude toward comedy, the way he delivered his lines that made him so unique . . . .

"Jack was a very special person in my life . . . ."

One of the reasons Johnny moved himself and *The Tonight Show* to Los Angeles was so he could be close to comedians and performers like Benny, whose professionalism and wit he admired. The tenth anniversary telecast of *The Tonight Show* from Los Angeles featured many of those comedians, including Bob Hope, Dean Martin, and George Gobel. Broadcast in October 1972, "It was," recalled Johnny, "just one of those nights when everything jelled.

"Bob was Bob, Dean stayed the whole show, where we thought he would leave after a few minutes. There were so many laughs, we were getting behind on commercials. Gobel finally walked on, when there were approximately fifteen minutes left to go, looking a little out of place in his old-fashioned crew-cut. His opening line was a classic: 'Did you ever get the feeling that the whole world's a tuxedo—and you're a pair of brown shoes?' The audience fell apart. In one pithy sentence, old Lonesome George toppled the mighty who had preceded him."

That show was followed by a memorable party at the Beverly Hills Hotel. It was one of the greatest nights of Johnny's show-biz life, and it made him feel secure about the move to Los Angeles. It was also a great day in his own life. That afternoon, on the tenth anniversary of *The Tonight Show*, he married his third wife, Joanna Holland.

In 1978, Johnny was named Man of the Year by Harvard's Hasty Pudding Club. For the visit, he stayed at Harvard's Eliot House and was greeted by students and faculty. To the left is the venerable John H. Finley, Jr., Master of Eliot House, renowned professor of the classics, and unabashed Carson fan.

Jimmy Stewart, demonstrating more Ivy League lore, shows Johnny a Princeton University cheer during a 1977 Tonight Show *appearance.*

Fred Silverman, then president of NBC, Joanna and Johnny putting the best possible face on things at a Friars Club dinner in Carson's honor in May, 1979. With relations between Carson and Silverman strained at the time, Johnny had intended to retire from The Tonight Show.

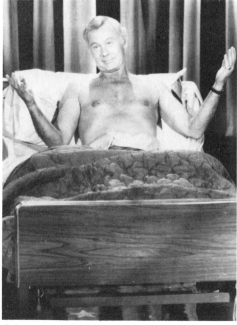

Johnny was wheeled on stage to start his seventeenth season. He said, "People seem to watch me while they are horizontal, so now I thought I'd do the monologue for them while I'm horizontal." His stage mark, the star, is visible under the bed.

From sailor suits to tailored suits. Johnny and Ed McMahon celebrated the twentieth anniversary of The Tonight Show *in 1982.*

Johnny and Joanna party with other Hollywood cowboys and girls. Although Johnny had lots of show biz pals, it was weird Beverly Hills parties like this that made him eager for a simpler life—at the beach.

After a publicized arrest in 1982 on drunken driving charges in Beverly Hills, Johnny appeared on the show accompanied by a "prop cop" to explain the incident. Support from his public far outweighed criticism from the press.

Doc Severinsen started with The Tonight Show *before* Johnny, working as a trumpet player for Skitch Henderson. He's been band leader—and sartorial foil—since 1967.

Johnny with twelve-days' growth. The beards never lasted long.

Carson's Characters—Johnny's comedic talent includes his clever parodies (clockwise from top right): L.A. Dodgers pitcher Fernando Valenzuela in a skit about diet drinks; President Reagan; Mister Liberty, in honor of the 100th anniversary celebrations of the statue; singer Willie Nelson in a spoof with Julio Iglesias; and movie character, John Rambo, in a sketch entitled "Mr. Rambo's Neighborhood."

Joanna and Johnny shortly before their separation in 1983.

Fred de Cordova, producer of The Tonight Show *since 1970, is always close to Carson, sitting just a few feet away from him on the show, and talking with him constantly by phone off the show.*

At a backstage birthday party for Johnny, Ed offers him a can of long-time sponsor's product, Alpo dog food, with a candle on top.

Carson, Judge Wapner, and David Letterman in a skit about a dispute over Letterman's truck.

Johnny's company owns and produces Late Night with David Letterman. *Here the boss sits in as a guest.*

Animal expert Jim Fowler appears several times a year on The Tonight Show. *Here he introduces Johnny to some large cats and a small marsupial.*

Johnny with Alexandra Mass. Once again he's with a rather private woman, leading a low-key lifestyle.

Johnny makes a fashion statement with pop singer Cyndi Lauper.

Ed and Johnny. Since 1962 the two have made The Tonight Show *work. They are still great friends, though they now lead rather separate lives.*

10
'I Want to Meet Her.'

J ohnny Carson met Joanna Holland in 1970 in New York, when he was going through a divorce from his second wife, Joanne Copeland. Their meeting has a movie-like charm, as related to us by Joanna.

"I was in the fashion business and was raising a little boy, my son Tim, who was seven when I met Johnny. I had been married from 1960 to 1966 to Tim Holland when we had divorced in a very amiable, civilized fashion.

"In 1970 I was doing what any female living in New York in 1970 was doing—trying to keep her act together while asking herself, 'Is having it all worth it?'

"But I loved my life. I loved being a model very much. I loved the activity, the creativity, and working with designers. In 1970 I was beginning to become more involved with fashion magazines, though, and with designers. I was starting to travel more. I was going to Milan to visit the silk mills and to buy fabrics. I was interested in getting involved with that side of fashion, the manufacturing side and the fashion magazine side. It seemed that in 1970, my life was taking a new turn in those directions. Then I met Johnny.

"How we met has been recorded in all the magazines and it is really a wonderful story. I met him at '21' [the famous New York speakeasy turned restaurant frequented by business, communications, and show business stars]. He was there having dinner with Jack and Mary Benny, Freddie de Cordova, and Molly Parnis. I had worked for Molly Parnis for years in the fashion business. I still call her my Jewish Mama. I have an Italian one, but I'm lucky, I have a Jewish one too.

"Anyway, I walked in and was with a man, but Johnny saw me and he asked Molly, 'Do you know who that lady is?' She looked and saw it was me. Johnny said, 'I want to meet her.' So Molly introduced us, and that was that.

"About a week later I went to '21' for lunch with a girlfriend, and Chuck, the headwaiter, said to me, 'My God, where have you been? Molly Parnis has been trying to reach you.' As it happened, I had just moved into a new apartment with my little boy and no one knew how to reach me, so I said, 'Well, I'll call her.' I thought it was fashion oriented, that she wanted me to do a show for her.

"So I called her, and she said, 'Oh, darling, why did it take you so long? This Johnny Carson has been calling me every day. He wants to meet you. May I give him your phone number?' Well, at that time he was going through this divorce that was headlines in the newspaper. So I was very reluctant. I said, 'No, I don't think so. I just don't think that's for me. I don't want to be involved.'

"But the very next day, he called me. And three weeks later, on his birthday, we had our first date. And after that first date, we talked to each other every single day for as long as I can remember.

"He seemed shy to me. Well, he seemed shy after having seen him on television for so many years, and then to be sitting with him, one on one. I found him entirely different than he appeared to be on that show. I found him a little insecure, a little shy.

"We dated for two years before we got married. After Johnny's divorce, and before we got married, we redecorated his apartment in New York at United Nations Plaza and did a beautiful job. That was in 1972.

"The apartment, before we redecorated it, seemed not complete. I can't explain this except to say it seemed as if nothing was completed there for Johnny. I really feel—maybe it's because I'm Italian—that when a man comes home, especially a man of his stature in the community, that the atmosphere should be quiet and peaceful. Things should be run the way he wants them run. It's my mother's training. And I always tried to do that for him. I worked with a decorator I knew in New York. Johnny likes earth colors, so it was very warm. We mixed old English end tables and accessories with overstuffed sofas and beautiful beiges and browns with rust tones, and very pretty carpeting. It was elegant, but it had so much warmth. When we did finish the apartment, it was fabulous, and we gave our first party there.

"Molly Parnis speaks of it often. Every major person was invited, and they all came to the party for Johnny. He just glowed in his new atmsophere. He was very happy. I was happy to share that experience with him. And then six months later, he decided he was moving *The Tonight Show* to Los Angeles! I nearly had a heart attack."

But, despite Joanna's initial shock, they were happy in Los Angeles, especially during the early years. And the move was good for the show. Johnny continued to build it into an institution cherished by viewers and marvelled at by show people. For entertainers, being on *The Tonight Show* is a sought-after and, needless to say, important experience.

More than thirty-four thousand people have been guests ("and thirty-two thousand of them have been Tony Randall," Johnny has joked) on *The Tonight Show* since Johnny began hosting it in 1962. Few, however, have ever spoken about their experience, except to say that it was somehow nerve wracking. Mariette Hartley, now of the *CBS Morning Show* says being on *The Tonight Show* is a "fantastic" adventure. "It's way up there," she says, "totally out of control, freewheeling and dangerous. The only thing I can compare it to is great sex."

Tom Snyder, who for awhile hosted NBC's post-*Tonight Show* program, found it literally uncomfortable. "You are sitting in this awful chair. I mean a chair that has got to be the most uncomfortable chair in the history of television. At the break I say, 'Johnny, is this chair uncomfortable on purpose?' He says, 'Yep. That's right. I need all the weapons I can get to keep people off guard.'"

Snyder, who felt the chair was too rough, did not understand why the furniture is so designed: Once, back in New York, when more luxurious seats were used, a guest fell asleep during the show. Hard seats were installed within days.

Cutting to a commercial is another device Johnny uses to keep the show lively. When a guest is proving to be less than scintillating, Johnny will sometimes yawn. The camera never shows his open mouth, but the guest and producer Fred de Cordova see it. If things don't liven up within seconds, de Cordova obligingly will signal Johnny to cut to a commercial. A new guest will follow.

The etiquette of talk-show appearances requires that once your moment in the special guest seat is over, you move quietly over to the couch, letting the new guest have his or her moment with Johnny. You also must, as TV technicians say, stay "out of the shot."

In other words, you don't try to insert yourself, by your behavior or by talking, into the camera shot of the new guest talking with Johnny. One night when Suzanne Pleshette, a relative newcomer, was on, the previous guest, the late gossip columnist Hedda Hopper, kept trying to get back into the action by patting Suzanne on the arm. During a commercial break, Pleshette turned to Hopper and snapped, "If you pat me on the arm again, I'm going to knock you on your can." The stunned Hopper pulled away and sat meekly by for the rest of the program. Carson was delighted by the incident and decided to invite the feisty Pleshette back often. She and Johnny have become good friends over the years (though they have never been linked romantically). Carson simply likes people who understand how the show works and make it work for them.

One aspect of *Tonight Show* ritual which sometimes confuses TV viewers is the treatment afforded young comedians who do stand-up routines, usually during the last half hour of the show. Some are invited to come up to the desk for a chat after they've done their bit. But most, no matter how hilarious, are not invited to the panel. Carson has explained why:

"It's decided beforehand. The [comedians'] agents don't like it . . . but we only let those whom the audience already knows sit down.

"If you're dismissed, it's not being cruel. It's what works for the show. The show's the point. Sometimes you have to do it that way.

"We create the show while it's on the air. It would be silly, as well, for me to say, if a comedian is working well, 'Now, we've got to stop this and bring out so and so, who's going to tell us how to make leather belts.' I don't want to wreck the pacing of the show."

What Carson, generously, does not mention is that few stand-up comics are good conversationalists. When they've finished their five or six minutes on stage, they've usually exhausted all their material and have nothing more to say. So it's often for the comics' own benefit, as well as for the show's and the audience's, that the newer comedians, no matter how funny, remain limited to their routines.

Over the years, Carson has had his ups and downs with some other comedians, including those who have appeared as guest hosts. Once, the late Dick Shawn, substituting for Johnny, destroyed Johnny's desk on camera. "I didn't go for that," Carson said. "It was just a sign of how desperate he was." And for awhile Shawn was *persona non grata* on *The Tonight Show*.

In the heyday of *Saturday Night Live*, there was an amazing rumor that Chevy Chase would be replacing Johnny as the host of *The Tonight Show*. The story, fueled by rumors that Johnny was about to retire, made no sense and Johnny was furious when he heard it. Fans of Chase pointed out that Chevy, during a stint as a guest host on *The Tonight Show*, ad-libbed well. "I said," Johnny later reported, "I didn't think Chevy Chase could ad-lib a fart after a baked bean dinner. I think [Chevy] took umbrage at that a little."

Around Hollywood, it was said that Shawn and Chase would never again appear on *The Tonight Show*. But Johnny is generous, especially towards other comedians. Both subsequently appeared often on the show, and Carson resumed his friendship with both. Shawn, during a career comeback, received a big boost from Johnny; and nowadays Chase and Carson play in a weekly poker game. Johnny really doesn't hold a grudge.

11
The Blockbuster Announcement

The ABC network and the producers of the Academy Awards show asked Johnny in 1978 to host the "Oscars." The invitation was a tribute to Johnny's towering celebrity. For the first time, the ceremonies of the movie business' annual fete to itself would be hosted by a television, not a movie, star. Though some of Tinseltown's old hands were appalled, the show's producers pointed out that, in the age of television, the surest way to draw attention to the movie industry and attract audiences to movie houses was to entertain them at home with a television star they really liked.

As Carson, in his easy-going way, mocked the length of the festivities ("Two hours of sparkling entertainment, spread out over four hours" was how he—on air—once described the Oscar show) and poked fun at the pretensions of some of the guests, he triumphed as the host. Ratings for the Academy Awards show rose, and Carson, not surprisingly, was asked back the following year to once again preside over the presentation of Oscar.

On that night in 1979 shrewd eyes in Hollywood thought they detected something more going on. Just as Johnny had wooed his first wife, Jody, while presiding over the 1948 University of Nebraska Women's Show in which she was a performer, someone was wooing Johnny Carson during the 1979 Oscar show in which he was the performer. The suitor, however, was not a lady. It was ABC.

Johnny, as host of the show, was only a guest of the ABC network; the NBC network held the primary interest in Carson's talents. But during and after the Oscar show, ABC tried to make Johnny understand that he could have a new home at ABC if ever he wanted one. In addition to lavish praise about his work on the show, ABC announcers, during the broadcast's commercial breaks, flattered Carson by further trumpeting his appearance on the show. And afterwards, in addition to his fee, Carson received an expensive ostrich-skin briefcase from the network. A mere bagatelle, perhaps, but one which would contribute to the show-business bombshell of the year.

Events leading up to the crisis had started the previous spring when NBC and Johnny signed a fabulous three-year contract that gave him about $3 million a year, fifteen weeks of vacation a year, and a three-day work week, except for four-day weeks during the February, May, and November ratings periods when the size of a TV show's audience is measured. While that contract seemed to leave Carson very happy, within a few months NBC officials were unhappy. Not only had *The Tonight Show*'s ratings begun to slip slightly under the three-day-a-week routine, but NBC's total profits were down by 20 percent. With a prime-time schedule that included such bombs as *Supertrain* (a quickly cancelled $12 million waste of network cash), *Sheriff Lobo, Mrs. Columbo, BJ and the Bear, Little Women, Brothers & Sisters,* and *Sweepstakes,* NBC was beginning to sink into the third and final place in the network race. NBC network president Fred Silverman, instead of tending to the prime-time schedule, began to put pressure on Carson.

He started a campaign to press Carson into taking less vacation time, while expanding his work week. As TV columnist Gary Deeb said at the time, "No one can fault Silverman for desiring that, but his methods are burning Johnny up."

Silverman, for example, in an interview with *Newsweek* magazine on March 19, 1979, said, "It doesn't take a mastermind to figure out that when Carson is on the program it does better than when he isn't on. He has a contract permitting him to make only three appearances each week, and that has only a couple more years to run. But I only hope that there will come a moment in time when he will say to himself, 'I love *The Tonight Show,* and I'm going to do a little bit more.' He's a very competitive and professional guy. I don't think he must enjoy reading that the thing is slipping."

Carson was furious at the treatment he was receiving from Silverman, and angry that Silverman had taken their dispute to the press. He responded in his usual way—with jokes—and for a few weeks his monologue and other remarks were strewn with anti-NBC and anti-Fred Silverman jokes. It was a bitter situation. In an interview with Mike Wallace for *60 Minutes,* Wallace quoted an instance when Silverman praised Carson, to which Carson answered sarcastically, "Awww, isn't that sweet."

Silverman also continued nudging Carson to book more NBC stars—often stars of failing shows—on *The Tonight Show.* Carson was upset at the network's attempt once again to use his show for promotional purposes at the expense of the quality of its entertainment. And ultimately, Carson was irked at NBC for the generally shoddy behavior it had shown him since the retirement in 1978 of Dave Tebet, an NBC executive who looked after the stars and listened to their complaints. With Tebet gone, there was no one to complain to. ABC sensed Carson's bruised feelings.

CBS, the other network, also shared in the fun. In an April interview prepared for CBS' *60 Minutes,* Carson dropped the bomb: he was quitting *The Tonight Show.* The NBC news people couldn't even find him for an interview.

The news couldn't have come at a worse time for NBC and the owners of its affiliated stations. The stock prices of RCA, NBC's corporate parent, dropped three-eighths of a point to twenty-seven dollars. The station owners, heading off for their annual meeting, were depressed. The *New York Times* headline of April 20 put it succinctly, "Carson Leaving 'Tonight Show': Setback to NBC."

What was worse, Carson told Silverman he wanted to leave quickly and not serve out the remaining two years on his contract. He wished to leave in September 1979, only five months away.

Finally, Carson did talk to NBC News about his decision: "I'm unhappy, obviously, for the network. I've been with them a long time, and obviously this does not come at a very good time for them. But as I told Mr. Silverman, I don't feel like Benedict Arnold, and I think that after seventeen years you can hardly be called a deserter. It was just a desire to leave earlier than the next two years. As to when that time will be, that's what we're going to have to meet about in the next few days."

In another interview Carson said he was "emotionally and intellectually tired and wanted to pursue other interests including prime-time variety shows, movies, and more personal appearances and concerts." After making these statements, he then went on a week's vacation, which was to have been followed by a meeting with Silverman, who had made a public appeal to Carson to stay with the show.

"Johnny was at a point," Joanna Carson said to us. "He wanted to do everything throughout his life. He was offered a lot of roles to star in movies. At that point, perhaps, he thought he needed a new challenge."

But there was also Johnny's awareness that there were other opportunities in television—ones that NBC, in its panicked state, could not think of offering. And although ABC executives have always denied they really talked business with Carson, it is generally believed that they not only offered him a chance to perform occasionally on variety shows and specials of his own design, but also a chance to become a major producer in his own right.

But why would a man like Johnny Carson, who was making $3 million a year from his television show alone, want to give that up?

The simple answer is that the television industry operates in a wild fashion, and that in becoming a producer and giving up the show, Johnny stood to make much more than the $5 million or so a year he was getting from his TV show and other investments.

In television, the *real* money—the tens of millions of dollars—is not made by performers but by the producers who put the programs together and rent them to the networks. After the networks have aired the shows an agreed-upon number of times, the producers have the right to sell the shows again—this time for stations to broadcast them five days a week in the daytime or late at night, instead of once a week in prime time. This practice, called "stripping," requires a show to have been such a hit in prime time that there are at least one hundred episodes available for sale. And when this can be done, it's very lucrative for the producers. The propietors and producers of *Magnum, P.I.,* for instance, sold the rights to rerun old episodes of the show to individual stations around the country for millions per episode.

And in Hollywood, the producers, not the stars, are the real royalty. Few Americans know the name Aaron Spelling, but as producer of *Dynasty, Loveboat,* and other shows, he is one of the most powerful and socially important men in Hollywood. Johnny was not unimportant in America, but in Hollywood, in 1979, he was merely an entertainer. To be at the top of the social ladder of Hollywood, Carson had to become a producer.

The additional advantage of being a producer—aside from the wealth, fame, and power which accrue—is that it's a post that doesn't necessarily require very much work. The prospect of even more free time appealed to Carson, who indeed was growing weary after seventeen years in the job, a job that always seemed to require playing tiresome politics with the network.

These were the concerns that were on Johnny's mind as NBC began antagonizing him while ABC was letting him know the latch was open. So he told NBC he wanted an early out from his contract. As *People* magazine wrote, "It doesn't take Karnak the Magnificent to guess what might be in the envelope ABC proferred Carson: whatever he wants."

While Carson was away, NBC execs began some maneuvering of their own. Typically, they were hamfisted: They would hold Johnny to his contract, "and we expect him to honor it," a network spokesman told the press. Johnny would not be let out early.

But the network also began secret talks with potential replacement hosts. Steve Martin had a meal with Fred Silverman but said he wasn't interested. Chevy Chase was also allegedly approached. Phil Donahue's name appeared on some network lists as did Tom Snyder's. Snyder, a bluff fellow with a hairdo that was as big as a bonnet, was then hosting a talk show on NBC following Carson's. He was said to be most interested in the job.

NBC also began investigating rumors that ABC's pursuit of Carson went beyond ostrich-skin briefcases, flowers, and on-air praise. Carson's contract with NBC apparently had a clause which forbade any significant talks between him and another network. NBC lawyers indicated they were ready to sue Carson and ABC.

But it was Fred de Cordova and a few other of Carson's old friends who actually achieved NBC's goals—and they did it without mean tactics and nasty threats. De Cordova and his wife talked with Joanna and Johnny, and after realizing that Carson was set in his purpose, de Cordova talked with Johnny yet again and reminded him of what he really believed: that the show was a great forum, and that there might be other ways to handle the problem.

Carson agreed, at any rate, that an angry departure wasn't the answer, and on May 2, 1979, when Carson returned from vacation, he had good news for his audience: he would stay on through the summer and fall, and maybe into the next year. The change of mind, he said, was "definitely not due to any pressure from network execs. I feel I owe it to the show and to NBC. I will definitely stay beyond October 1, and I may stay longer, possibly into 1980."

In the same announcement, he touched on other feelings which indicated things were far from resolution. "I have terribly ambivalent feelings. I don't want the show to become boring. I want to keep it at a professional level."

Many people associated with Carson breathed more easily that night, but not Tom Snyder, who was said to have been devastated. Although Johnny's remarks indicated that he was still troubled, they also indicated that Carson the showman had won out for a moment over both the tired Carson and the Carson who sought to be an even bigger businessman.

Referring to his change of heart, he joked, in that gas-line-clogged spring, that he had changed his mind only for the promise from Fred Silverman of a steady supply of gasoline.

In early May, Carson was the roastee at a Friars Club dinner in New York attended not only by Fred Silverman but also by the Egyptian and Israeli ambassadors to the United States. Bob Hope quipped, "Having the Israeli and Egyptian ambassadors here is a plot to show Freddie and Johnny it can be done."

The dinner lasted over four hours, leading Hope to remark, "All the NBC brass is here, refilling Johnny's wine glass, cutting his steak, kissing his ring—they never did get any dinner, they kept ordering and cancelling, ordering and cancelling, ordering and cancelling.

"I admire a man," said Hope, "who can do what John has done to his network as many times, as many ways, and in as many positions. Next year he's got a sweeter deal: $43 million and he only has to show up once a week to pick up his messages."

Fred Silverman reported to interviewers after the roast that "slow progress" was being made in the talks to make things more comfortable for Johnny. But Carson told Kay Gardella, the respected TV reporter of the New York *Daily News,* that he still had ambivalent feelings, and he gave a hint of things to come when he told Gardella, "No one can force a performer to work. After seventeen years, six hours a week, I do feel I have nothing left to give to the program."

He would soon be off on another vacation, this time to Europe. Before going to London to see the Wimbledon tennis matches, he and Joanna stopped in the south of France. And who should be staying, not only in the same hotel, but in the same corridor? ABC executives Elton Rule, Gary Pudney, and Fred Pierce. The Carsons and the ABC executives went sailing together.

Joanna Carson recollects: "We were all in the south of France. That whole group from ABC—Elton Rule, who was the chairman; Tony Thomopolous, the president—came down from England and we spent four or five days together.

"But I don't think they were 'wooing' Johnny. I think they made it known if he were interested in changing networks, they were interested in having him. And they wanted also for him to do the Academy Awards. When Johnny decided to stay with NBC, it was the right decision because when you're 'king of the network,' you don't switch in midstream.

"And Johnny, like me, ultimately was a loyal person. He felt they [the network] stuck by it [the show]. They had been good to him. They hadn't refused him anything that he wanted. Negotiations are always tough, and we loved the group from ABC a lot. We're still friends with them and they're very close, but they got him for the Academy Awards.

"And when you see how history has turned around on ABC, it was the right decision to make. Johnny always made the right decision when it came to his career."

12
Bombastic
Bushkin

"**H**enry Bushkin is a better tennis player than he is a lawyer." That is the jocular opinion of one television producer who, in the course of dealing with Johnny Carson's production company, has had to deal with Bushkin, who is Johnny's extraordinarily powerful attorney. Clearly, Johnny does not agree with the producer's opinion. In the summer of 1979, when Carson was negotiating his announced departure from NBC, it was Bushkin who represented Carson in both legal and business matters. And NBC, which wasn't the least bit interested in the quality of his tennis game, found Bushkin sharp enough. Fierce in his representation of Johnny's interests, Bushkin was more than Johnny's lawyer; he was also Johnny Carson's best friend.

The Nebraska comedian and the Beverly Hills lawyer, one silver-haired and smiling, the other dark-haired and suspicious, were an unlikely combo as pals. But in a town where people cynically refer to someone they've met only in a restaurant foyer as "a close, personal friend," the friendship between Johnny Carson and Henry Bushkin was genuine and solid. Carson indeed trusted Bushkin with the management of his money. What Sonny Werblin had started to do years ago in New York—make Johnny a wealthy man—Bushkin continued to do in Los Angeles. And Bushkin, due to his famous friend, had become famous in his own right.

Millions of Americans frequently heard Johnny refer to "Bombastic Bushkin" in the course of his monologue, though few probably realized that the man with the comic name, who apparently kept trying to get Johnny to invest in such sure-fire failures as "Ronald Reagan Memory Schools," was not only a real person but also Johnny's friend, financial advisor, lawyer, and frequent tennis partner. To those who knew Bushkin, however—including the hundreds of people who either do business with Johnny Carson, or who wanted to do business with him—Bushkin was very real and anything but a comic figure.

He moved Johnny from the world of celebrity endorsements into the world of big business, where the deals are so complicated, involving downsides and upsides so arcane, that only a Beverly Hills lawyer could figure them out. For the most part Bushkin did his job well, though not everything worked well. And the "Johnny Carson bank" episode and the failed attempt to take over the Alladin Hotel in Las Vegas were two enterprises that must have contributed to Johnny's sense of fatigue in 1979.

Early in that year, newspapers announced that Johnny Carson, along with four other investors, including Henry Bushkin, had acquired a 94 percent interest in a bank called the Garden State Bank of Hawaiian Gardens, a bank which was neither in New Jersey, the garden state, nor in Hawaii, but rather—coincidentally enough—on Carson Street in a small industrial suburb far south of Los Angeles, not only far from Hawaii but also light years from Beverly Hills, Bel-Air, and Burbank.

In the deal, which was orchestrated by Bushkin, the bank said "aloha" to its old name, its Mexican-American customers, and its drab neighborhood. Renaming itself the Commercial Bank of California, it opened a new office on Sunset Boulevard amidst the offices of television and recording companies, theatrical agents, and actors' business managers. Carson, who paid $1,950,000 for his shares, became the bank's chairman and attended the first two board meetings. Expensive parties followed, with a picture of Johnny at one such party being printed in *Playboy*. In its beginnings, Johnny's bank did not appear to be like other banks. That was what the federal government apparently thought as well.

Within three years, the Federal Deposit Insurance Corporation (FDIC), the government sponsored insurer of banks, accused Johnny, Bushkin, and other bank officials of allowing loans to be made to people "associated directly or indirectly with organized crime." Bushkin promptly replied that Carson, in fact, had little or nothing to do with the operation of the bank, and certainly had nothing to do with the activities which had upset the FDIC.

Eventually, the matter would straighten itself out, with Johnny vindicated. Bushkin and the others who had come up with the Hawaiian Gardens idea probably had sound business objectives

165

in mind, but their management of the situation resulted in embarrassing and excruciating litigation. And Johnny, who had been really just a figurehead and who had only attended the first two board meetings, was caught up in the mess. The disappointing and in some ways humiliating end, however, did not terminate the relationship between Johnny and Bushkin, who, in the meantime, was hard at work dealing with NBC over Johnny's desire to leave the show.

At the time NBC was insisting that Johnny serve the full term of his contract. Bushkin, in response, located an obscure provision of California law that forbade contracts longer than seven years between a performer and a company, but its application in Carson's case was very unclear, given that Johnny had repeatedly signed several short-term contracts with NBC, not one long seven-year one. As this matter was quickly put before a special judge, other problems with business deals arose.

Johnny had wanted to buy the troubled Aladdin Hotel in Las Vegas and had endured prolonged negotiations to do so. Finally the deal fell through when Johnny's group couldn't obtain approval from local authorities. Then Wayne Newton, the singer who had been the frequent butt of Carson's jokes because of his falsetto voice, suddenly ended up owning the Aladdin. Carson sensed politics. Newton, it was said, had entered the Aladdin situation just to frustrate Johnny and pay him back for the years of jokes. When Carson learned that Newton would get the hotel, he was so angry, columnist Liz Smith reported, that he wasn't able to speak without his own voice quivering. While Newton has yet to return to *The Tonight Show* as a guest (his last appearance was in 1979), Johnny's jokes about Newton have also stopped.

Of all his extra-show-business enterprises, only the Johnny

Carson Apparel Company, of which he is the president, seemed to bring him pleasure and profit. It was also the one outside business he had in which he was actively involved.

A division of the massive Hart, Schaffner & Marx menswear business, the Johnny Carson Apparel Company was founded in 1970, when the clothiers recognized that Johnny was a celebrity clothes horse who was not so *outre* as to offend middle America.

The clothes Johnny wears on the air are always stocked in the stores, and with Johnny's help, they become the company's best sellers.

He never wears samples or models not already in the market. "Nothing could be worse," says a Hart, Schaffner & Marx representative, "than to have a customer walk in and describe a jacket he saw Johnny wearing on TV the night before, only to have us tell him we haven't got it, or it isn't yet available. Carson insists it be there."

Four times a year, Johnny meets with the officers of his company and goes over the designs and colors that are being chosen for the next season. He has veto power over items and frequently cancels designs, fabrics, and colors he doesn't like. Clothes that are too wild, and colors that are too outrageous are nixed—though he doesn't hold the company to his own two favorite colors, blue and gray.

While the clothing company specializes in ready-to-wear clothes, Carson must have his clothes specially made. Not out of vanity, but because of his unusual build. He has a thirty-two-inch waist and a body builder's forty-one-inch chest. When the tailors cut a suit for Carson to wear on the air, they also cut an identical version for him to wear at home, where he keeps about fifty suits in his wardrobe. They are added to and deleted from about once a month.

The big news of the autumn of 1979, however, was not about Johnny's bumpy business life, nor about his efforts to get out of his NBC contract, but about a revelation concerning his personal life he made on the CBS program *60 Minutes.* It was here that Johnny spoke about his drinking, confirming the stories that had been drifting around over the years, ever since he had moved to New York. It was a manly admission.

"When I did drink," Carson told interviewer Mike Wallace, "rather than a lot of people who become fun loving and gregarious and love everybody, I would go just the opposite. And it would happen just like that. I just found out that I didn't drink well. That's one reason I found that it was probably best for me not to tangle with it."

That autumn, besieged with contract and business problems, he seemed in private a sad, troubled, tired man. "I would see him in the daytime," says the wife of a business associate, "and he would just seem gray. Then at night on the show, he'd manage to sparkle."

A few days after Thanksgiving, he told a story about the state of foreign affairs that seemed to reflect on his own beleagured status. "President Carter," Johnny joked, "had celebrated Thanksgiving by phoning the leaders of every country in the world that supports the United States and . . . ran up a phone bill of thirty-five cents."

Bushkin kept battling away with NBC, however, and on May 7, 1980, just about a year after Carson had asked Bombastic Bushkin to find a way for him to quit *The Tonight Show*, there was the startling news that Johnny had signed a *new* contract with NBC, even as a judge was trying to figure out if he could walk out of his old one.

New York's *Daily News* explained: "The Johnny Carson-NBC

poker game has ended and Carson walked with the pot. After months of haggling and rumors of a move to ABC, it was announced yesterday that Carson has signed a three-year contract."

Everyone was baffled. Why had Johnny, who seemed so eager to quit, signed a contract committing himself to an additional three years on the show?

In part, the answer lay in the business confusions of the previous year. The bank, the Aladdin hotel, and other deals had taken their toll. A year previously Johnny may have thought that he wanted to spend more time on new businesses, but the heartache and confusion they produced apparently helped to convince him to concentrate on show business, the area that he really knew well.

The problem was to work out an arrangement by which he could enjoy the show, which still would require a great deal of effort, while expanding his entertainment-related activities. Business interests outside of show business may have turned sour, but he knew he could make substantial money not only as a TV star but also as a producer.

Over the months, secretly, Carson's lawyers and NBC's lawyers had tried to figure out a way to achieve these goals. Finally they came up with a contract that satisfied both sides.

Johnny would return to *The Tonight Show* four nights a week, as Silverman had wished. But the length of the show would be cut from ninety minutes to sixty minutes.

Johnny would also receive a salary of about $6 million for hosting *The Tonight Show*.

To satisfy Johnny's ambition to be a producer, NBC agreed to provide Carson with $12 million to fund Carson Productions, which would not only produce *The Tonight Show* and other TV shows, but also movies. In the future *The Big Chill*, the celebrated story of yuppie life, would be Carson Productions' biggest movie hit; *Late Night with David Letterman,* which would replace *The Tom Snyder Show*, following *The Tonight Show,* would become its biggest television hit.

After the new contract was announced, Johnny appeared before a studio audience that wouldn't stop applauding until he shushed them and said: "There are about four billion people on this planet. About three billion, eight hundred million don't know who I am or what I do, and couldn't care less."

Then he joked that Fred Silverman had tricked him into signing the new contract by telling him it was a petition to get *Sheriff Lobo* off the air.

That evening's show had been delayed for the presentation of an NBC news special about the day's presidential primaries. For once, Carson didn't mind being pre-empted. He loved the craziness of politics, and with his contracts settled and a presidential campaign to look forward to, he was as bright and amusing as ever.

The newspapers were again quoting Carson as the barometer of American feeling.

In October, at the height of the election campaign between Jimmy Carter, Ronald Reagan, and the now forgotten independent, John Anderson, the *New York Times* remarked, "Johnny Carson, host of *The Tonight Show* . . . perhaps the nation's most prominent political commentator, demonstrated that Thursday night. He asked his studio audience if it thought Mr. Anderson should withdraw. A sizable portion applauded. Then Mr. Carson asked, 'How many think Carter and Reagan should withdraw?' Almost everyone clapped."

Later in the campaign, Johnny, in his monologue, would repeat

Reagan's remark that if all the unemployed were lined up, they would stretch from New York to Los Angeles. Carson then said, "[Reagan] came up with another one: if everyone on welfare were chopped liver, you could spread them on a line of Ritz crackers from here to Bulgaria." The audience went wild. Carson's closing remark was, "We've got to make a choice. And I think it's a clear-cut choice. Who do you want running our nation for the next four years? Nancy or Amy?"

The Reagans took the jokes well. When the election was over and done with, they welcomed Johnny as master of ceremonies at their inaugural festivities in Washington.

Meanwhile, Carson Productions was establishing itself in Hollywood. One of the very first hired was Dave Tebet, whose retirement from NBC as vice-president had preceded the bad blood which developed between Carson and Silverman. Carson Productions also announced plans for a new show which would follow Carson's own. It would star a protégé of Johnny's, and a frequent guest host on *The Tonight Show:* David Letterman.

But there was distressing news that winter, which pointed to the dark side of celebrity. In Los Angeles, December 1980 had been a happy holiday season, as the show-business world celebrated the election of one of its own to the presidency of the United States. Then one night, while the parties were tinkling along in Bel-Air and Beverly Hills, there came news that chilled entertainers all over Hollywood.

That early December night, John Lennon was murdered outside his apartment house in New York City. The shooting provoked fear in many, including Carson, who like Lennon had always prided himself on his ability to move about freely and without bodyguards. After the Lennon shooting, Carson tightened up his own security.

171

CARSON

"If you only knew the times," he told columnist and confidante Marilyn Beck, "I've had people tail me for miles right up to the driveway of my house. Sure, they probably are fans, but they could be dopers, even murderers, and you feel panic, absolute terror. It's a hell of a way to live."

So Johnny moved into the eighties with old problems resolved and new problems taking their place. He was leaving bad business deals behind; the contract problems with the network had been settled; and his monologues sparkled with sprightly, topical jokes. Yet he was suddenly fearful for his personal safety, and though he didn't seem to realize it yet, he was under enormous, almost suffocating, pressure in his private life.

13
Killer Labels

B y the early eighties, Johnny was trying to exist in two competing worlds, each of which was so busy that the friction between them was almost enough to burn him up. For one, there was the show. For years, Johnny's day had been structured around it: his mornings, noons, afternoons, and even post-performance evenings all had been geared to giving him the energy to do the show well. But he also had to satisfy the Beverly Hills—Bel-Air lifestyle of the stars, which in an earlier period had fascinated him.

When in 1978 he had had his contract rewritten to permit him to appear just three nights a week, the idea had been in part to give Joanna and Johnny more time to be together and to go out. Joanna was extremely active in the Beverly Hills social whirl, an exclusive tornado made up of women whose husbands have incomes in the millions of dollars a month, not a year.

Many of these women travel in small packs, lunching daily with one another at restaurants like the Bistro ("Beast-row" as the gossip columnists privately call it), Le Dome on the Sunset Strip, and La Scala on Little Santa Monica Boulevard in Beverly Hills.

The ladies' lives are built around shopping, entertaining, and charity work. "It's a cutthroat world," a Beverly Hills psychiatrist once told me. "These women are under enormous pressure to compete with one another in looks, in places on charity boards, and in entertaining."

Not to be named to the correct charity boards can be wounding. For example, the wife of the producer of one top-rated television show desperately wanted to be made a member of a group called the Amazing Blue Ribbon, which helps the good work of the Los Angeles Music Center. Her efforts were unavailing until she persuaded her husband to give a small walk-on role in his TV show to an Amazing Blue Ribbon officer. He agreed, the officer took the role, and the producer's wife was invited to join the Amazing Blue Ribbon.

"Beverly Hills is infested with the same kind of petty social climbing and snobbery that exists in every little city that has a country club," says the psychiatrist, "except in Beverly Hills the financial stakes are higher, the emotional hurt deeper, and the silliness more extreme."

Joanna Carson moved quickly to the top of this world, becoming active in Beverly Hills' most desirable charity group, SHARE (Share Happily And Reap Endlessly), which does do highly commendable work for retarded children through an annual show featuring the celebrity spouse members. Joanna, who loved being involved, moved through this world with such aplomb and verve that most people in Beverly Hills were surprised to learn that she was not native to the place and, in fact, had originally resisted moving to California with Johnny.

"Johnny had to push and shove to get her to come to California in 1972," a friend recalls. "Joanna insisted she wouldn't like it, but she took to the life very well."

Perhaps too well, because the celebrity circuit is never ending, and can be exhausting.

By 1981, Johnny, though still in love with Joanna, was balking at the demands made on him by her new-found social life. On May 25, 1981, at Joanna's request, Johnny performed as master of ceremonies at a SHARE dinner. He told the crowd, "I was invited here in the same manner that Agnew was invited to return the money." And Joanna was watching Johnny change.

"Around 1980," she told us, "I began to see things in our marriage that I didn't understand. Changes in Johnny that I didn't understand."

Not surprisingly there were rumors of stress in the marriage, and rumors that the couple might separate. But when the *National Enquirer* in 1981 printed a story saying the Carson marriage was in trouble, Johnny exploded. He brought the newspaper with him on the show, and made one of the few non-jocular statements he has ever made about his family on the air. Carson, whose remarks made headlines for days afterwards, said:

"I hope you will indulge me in a few minutes of some personal comment. I have ambivalent feelings about what I'm going to say, and it has to do with the *National Enquirer*. Somebody today handed me a copy of the *National Enquirer*.

"The reason I have ambivalent feelings about it is that I'm

giving publicity to the publication of which I think stinks, number one. And the possibility I will give them more publicity and people will read the article whom otherwise might not have seen it.

"On the cover is my picture. Inside, the headline says 'Johnny Carson Marriage in Serious Trouble.' It says 'close friends say he and his wife Joanna are headed straight for divorce.'

"I have not seen this until this morning. Now, before I get into this or say any more, I want to go on record right here in front of the American public because this is the only forum I have. They have this publication, and I have this show.

"This is absolutely, completely, 100 percent falsehood. It's untrue for openers. I guess I should be used to this kind of stuff, being in the entertainment business as long as I have, but they also attacked my wife in this particular article.

"They said some very nasty things, attributed to her, again, close friends and pals. And when they attacked my wife, then I get a little bit angry . . . .

"Now I could sue the *National Enquirer*. I'm not going to sue the *National Enquirer* because I do not want to go through the four or five years of litigation in which they call friends in and sources and put them through the mills. If you've ever been in deposition for this kind of thing, it's a very laborious task to go through.

"I'm not going to put my wife through it. My wife is a wonderful person. The comments they have made about her are completely untrue.

"The only reason I'm mentioning this, the people who want to believe it, fine. I don't care. But our friends, our relatives, our family, our children, our parents who read something like this . . . we've got calls already from all over the country, saying,

'I understand you're headed . . .' because they say you're going to get a divorce, and they go through a lot of other crap I'm not going to read to you.

"I'm going to call the *National Enquirer* and the people who wrote this, liars. Now that's slander. They can sue me for slander. You know where I am, gentlemen.

"Please accept my invitation for calling you liars. I've done it publicly now in front of fifteen or twenty million people and I will be very happy to defend that charge against you."

The studio audience applauded vigorously, and Carson then dropped the subject. Around town it was generally believed, however, that while the *Enquirer* may have gotten details wrong, they were close to the truth. But the *Enquirer* never sued for slander.

Johnny's remarks indicate, of course, that he was very concerned about the effect that stories about him had on his family. Johnny did not want problems in his personal life, but when there were problems, he did not want his family to be involved. His parents were still alive in 1981 and in their eighties. Stories about more marital trouble in his life troubled them, and he was upset that they were upset. By this time they had moved from Nebraska to a home in Scottsdale, Arizona, that Johnny had purchased for them, and which Joanna had decorated.

Johnny was also close to his brother, Dick, then the director of *The Merv Griffin Show,* and to his sister, Catherine Sozting, who had moved from Philadelphia to Monterey, California. Johnny had generously given Catherine's son, Jeff, a start in the TV business, helping him obtain a job to learn the behind-the-scenes aspects of television.

Though none of his own boys had shown an interest in becoming comedians or television stars, and though they were sometimes distant, as Joanna discusses in upcoming chapters, Johnny did keep in touch with them and helped them financially. The eldest, Chris, was a professional golfer living in Fort Lauderdale; Ricky was in California working as a musician; and Cory, the youngest, was working in the production side of television. To the extent that it was possible, Johnny sought to avoid burdening his boys with his problems or his celebrity. "I wanted to avoid that killer label, 'Johnny Carson, Junior,' " he once said. "It's monstrous and egomaniacal to call your kids junior." And he also never pressured them to go on the stage.

But, as he sought to shelter others, his own life showed further signs of tension in 1982. Early in March, when he and Joanna were driving home in his Delorean from an Italian restaurant, he was stopped by two Beverly Hills police officers who noticed that his license tag had expired.

The two policemen—Officers Angel and Foley—then asked Johnny to submit to a field sobriety test. He was asked to take a walking test. The police wrote that Johnny "lost balance, stumbled."

He was then asked to recite the alphabet. According to the police he "mumbled A, B, C, D, E, F . . . too garbled to understand the rest."

They then asked him to take a chemical breath test. "No, I'm not going to take any test," the police quoted him as saying at first. "You didn't prove anything by this. What did I do wrong? Tell me."

Within a few minutes though, he agreed to take the test, which indicated the level of alcohol in his blood was .16 mililiters, well above the official intoxication level of .10. Subsequently he was charged with driving under the influence of alcohol, not having a driver's license in his possession, and not having a valid automobile registration sticker on his car.

The arrest made headlines over the weekend. And when Carson appeared again on *The Tonight Show* on the following Tuesday, he did so with a "prop cop" in tow. Carson was extremely nervous about the audience's reaction, and was pleasantly startled to find that he was greeted with warm, sympathetic applause.

"You don't know how nice that sounds. Would you like to be my character witnesses?"

"For those of you watching this at home, please do not adjust the color in your set, that is just me blushing. This is what you call a slow news weekend. It probably would be impossible for me to do this whole show tonight without saying something about what has happened. I assume you know there has been a great deal of publicity that was given to a reported encounter between the law and me over the weekend.

"The true facts are probably not as exciting as what you may have heard. I had dinner with my wife Joanna and friends at a local restaurant, and I was stopped, I guess two blocks from the restaurant, for not having a 1982 sticker on my car, and subsequent to that, I complied with every request made by the police, which included a test to determine whether too much wine had been consumed with our dinner.

"That's really all the further I want to go with it except to say that I regret the incident, and I'll tell you one thing—you will never see me do that again."

His audience responded warmly. The law did not. On October 25 he was sentenced to three years' probation and fined $605. His license was restricted, allowing him for the next ninety days to drive only to and from work and to and from a required course on drinking and driving.

Jim Brady, the shrewd New York columnist, noted the most intriguing aspect of the mess—which was that on the date of Johnny's court arraignment, Joanna was not with him in Los Angeles. She was in New York at a party.

That marriage, and the Beverly Hills lifestyle, would soon be at an end.

14

'What I'll Miss the Most...'

I n the months between October 1982 and January 1983 the ten-year-old marriage of Joanna and Johnny Carson whimpered to its death. By March, it belonged to the lawyers. Now, it is one for the books. In this chapter, we present an account of the turmoil that surrounded their divorce. In the next chapter, in an exclusive interview, Joanna Carson presents a startling and fascinating view of her marriage with Johnny and her view of their divorce.

That their marriage lasted as long as it did is probably a tribute to both partners and their affection for one another. That it lasted much beyond 1981 is remarkable.

By that time Johnny Carson had apparently tired of the hectic pace of Beverly Hills society, while Joanna was still very much involved. Presiding over her charity boards, Joanna had come a long way from New York's Seventh Avenue, where she had started out as a model in the garment district. In the early eighties she was a regular in the social pages. A column in the *Hollywood Reporter* devoted to the celebration of the monied Beverly Hills lifestyle, and modestly entitled "The Great Life," constantly referred to Joanna as the woman with "the sexiest strut this side of Montmartre." In fact, she is stunningly beautiful rather than street-sexy, but the point of the *Reporter's* tag is not its aptness nor its accuracy, but that she was so famous in her own right, and was referred to so often in the column, that author George Christy granted her a title just as he had done for her friend, Janet de Cordova, Freddie's wife, who was dubbed "the duchess of Trousdale" (Trousdale Estates being her chic Beverly Hills neighborhood). Joanna was part of Society, and she seemed to love every Gucci-filled minute of it.

Johnny, of course, was also a member of that bizarre world devoted to endless black-tie testimonial dinners, the constant "gifting" of people with expensive gee-gaws, and other forms of dubious tribute designed to enhance one's standing in the social ramble. He had wanted that life. Indeed, that had been one of the benefits of moving *The Tonight Show* to Los Angeles in 1972. And, according to friends, to participate better in that life had been one of the reasons he had married Joanna Holland in the Beverly Hills Hotel on the very day, in 1972, *The Tonight Show* celebrated its tenth anniversary.

But there were signs that Johnny was less than entranced with having to go off to the fair every night. This was when Johnny as the emcee at a SHARE dinner made it clear he would have preferred to be elsewhere.

And at all of these events, so adored by Joanna, Johnny began to seem at best uncomfortable, as shown by a photograph (see photo section) of him dressed in a cowboy costume at a charity affair with Frank Sinatra.

The man who uttered the extraordinarily irreverent jokes on the monologue each night seemed not to be the same man whose name was mentioned every day in the society columns along with scores of humorless social climbers. Sometimes—though never on the show—he became as humorless as the rest of them.

And yet Johnny could still be the wide-eyed country boy. He was thrilled when NBC wanted to give him a $10,000 satellite dish for his seventeenth anniversary with the network. But when Joanna heard that the large antenna would be placed in the yard of their St. Cloud Drive home in Bel-Air, she was furious and said she wouldn't have anything so ugly on the grounds. Johnny gave in, and instead of the satellite dish, NBC presented him with a lump of antique amethyst.

Joanna Holland had been a hard-working model and society wife before she met Johnny in 1970 at the "21" Club in New York, and he was taken not only with her looks but with her style and panache. When Johnny wanted to move from New York to California, she resisted, thinking California was just too tacky. But once there she soon discovered her own world of society and power.

She also introduced Johnny to a more sophisticated lifestyle. Before meeting Joanna, for example, Johnny had never really travelled in Europe. But after they were married, Joanna took him to the south of France and England every spring for tennis and the social life. The boy from Nebraska seemed to like it a lot.

"Joanna probably has been one of the most positive influences in his life," says Joanna's friend Marjorie Reed. "She's made elegant homes for him to live very quietly, very graciously." And says Molly Parnis, who introduced the two, "Joanna was much more sophisticated than Johnny."

Johnny, in turn, gave Joanna not only enormous social position and a massive allowance, but also a great deal of freedom. Says Jody Wolcott Carson, Johnny's first wife, of wife number three, "She lived a very independent life, compared to me. Johnny did allow her to have a job of sorts—that of a fashion designer." And in 1981, Joanna became a partner of dress designer Michael Vollbracht.

Comments Jan Sarnoff, a prominent Beverly Hills resident, "An awful lot of people could be very jealous of Joanna—she's beautiful, brilliant, and is very loyal. She has many accomplishments—Woman of the Year awards, that sort of thing. She's also very organized and is a fantastic businesswoman. As president of SHARE, she was terrific. Of course, I'm partial to achievers—people who get things done rather than just talk. Joanna is one. She took care of every detail, even to getting down on her hands and knees in sweats and without make-up and making sure everyone's hem was even on our costumes for our annual show."

Another friend, who chooses not to be named, has different memories. "Joanna is Sicilian," he says "a bundle of emotion. She can be very sweet or very rough. She was always determined to be somebody. In SHARE it was the same thing. She was determined to become president of SHARE, and she did. She's very domineering, even a little cynical . . . . Alexandra Mass is just the opposite."

"I remember," says a friend, "an episode a few years ago that illustrates Joanna's domineering streak. It was at a SHARE party. Johnny was to be the master of ceremonies, and Governor Jerry

Brown was outside the building and was delayed coming in. Joanna made Johnny stand there on stage for twenty minutes, with really nothing to do, until Brown made his entrance. He could have sat down. But Joanna wouldn't let him. She wanted him standing for the governor. He looked glum. She just held on to him, and made him stand there, until Brown came in. He looked foolish. But it was the sort of thing she'd do. She's tough and liked wielding power."

Life with Joanna was a life that revolved around parties. Johnny seemed eventually to resent that. "He just doesn't like parties," says a friend and colleague. "Don't ask me why. He just doesn't. He got tired of them."

And there were other factors. During 1979, a tough year when Johnny not only had protracted problems with NBC, but also had to deal with ABC, which was interested in him, the social whirl was draining his energy and proving to be hazardous as well. The Securities and Exchange Commission, the government agency which oversees the stock market, for example, filed a lawsuit.

As the *Wall Street Journal* put it, "The Securities and Exchange Commission says it has discovered something NBC network executives have known for years: when Johnny Carson speaks, people listen."

The SEC alleged that when Johnny and the National Kinney Company were thinking about buying the Aladdin Hotel in Las Vegas, people close to Joanna Carson heard about the plans. The SEC filed a suit in federal court in New York charging that Joanna Carson told a masseuse at her health club and her brother about the impending deal, and that the wife of Johnny's lawyer, Henry Bushkin, told her father as well. The brother, masseuse and Bushkin's wife's dad all bought National Kinney stock and made profits in a hurry. They—but not Johnny—were accused, along with another lawyer, of breaking federal law by trading on inside information.

According to published reports of the SEC's suit, here's what was alleged:

Peter Ulrich of West Seneca, N.Y., a brother of Joanna Carson, bought two thousand shares of National Kinney on October 23, 1979, after Joanna, without Johnny's knowledge, told her brother about the potential deal with National Kinney. Ulrich later sold the stock and made a profit of $4,228. At Ulrich's request, according to the SEC, his mother and aunt also bought a total of 1,500 Kinney shares, but held on to them and didn't make a profit. Emily Johns, the masseuse who worked at the Beverly Hills health club and beauty salon where Joanna frequently went, bought herself one thousand shares of National Kinney on the same day, which happened to be the day after she and Joanna discussed the possible Kinney deal. Miss Johns made a profit of $1,260 when she sold the stock. While the four involved admitted no wrongdoing, they settled the suit by agreeing to pay back the profits they had made.

Apparently, Johnny was upset not only with the fact that the SEC said his wife's masseuse had tried to make a stock killing from remarks made by his wife on the kneading table, but also by the lifestyle that surrounded such activity.

While Johnny had his problems, Joanna had hers. Johnny, according to Joanna's friends, wasn't always so easy to live with. "He did resist her efforts to have him move about on the party circuit after awhile," says one of her SHARE friends, "and that upset her."

To the outside world the problems in the Carson marriage were primarily problems of lifestyle. Said one friend of Joanna,

"Johnny, off-stage, is a Nebraska yokel . . . and Joanna is a very sophisticated lady. He couldn't keep up with her." Says Richard Fischoff, a former Carson employee, "Johnny's temperament is very guarded. His behavior is not midwestern anymore, but he is very midwestern at heart. His basic values were shaped as a boy."

A well-known social figure in Beverly Hills adds, "Johnny and Joanna were wonderful together. I think it was just that Joanna liked to go out a lot and Johnny didn't—it could have been as simple as that. And why shouldn't she like to go out—she's gorgeous."

One of Johnny's oldest friends, who like most everyone associated with him will not speak for attribution, concurs:

"The problem with Joanna is that she loved parties and Johnny hated them. Now, his current girlfriend [now his wife] likes everything he likes. Johnny isn't reclusive, he's just a bit of a loner. He loves astronomy and has a couple of telescopes in his living room. He also has a complete Nautilus gym and works out every day. He loves to read. He's a big reader. And he loves going to art shows. But most of all he loves *The Tonight Show*. Being out every night took away from the energy. I thought they might have reconciled, but . . . "

Joanna also thought they might have reconciled. She told us that problems—issues which she won't name—had arisen in their marriage. "Johnny," she says, "would discuss the issues. We just couldn't resolve them. I used to say to him, 'If you would devote as much time to our relationship, our marriage, to your family, as you devote to that show, you couldn't help but have a 'hit' on your hands . . . .

"It was a very good marriage for most of the time. He used to talk about it on the show all the time—'This was it.' But we

187

just couldn't resolve the problems that arose. I think we tried for a year and a half, and ultimately I didn't want to lose respect for myself and wake up in the morning and not like me, because I like me a lot . . . . I think somewhere along the way, you try so hard, you try to resolve things when . . . I just kind of lost respect for him.

"I think that's what happened to me.

"So I made the decision that this marriage was not going anywhere, was not continuing in the manner it should, especially with all the time put into it! So I asked Johnny to leave the house, to go to our beach house and stay there. I think there was a certain shock, a certain anger—it hurts the male ego—and that's when the stories started that the whole thing was about money. That's when the press started perceiving me as greedy, as going after the pockets of the man that I loved. That was outrageous. Money was never even a subject that came up in our marriage. It hurt me badly; money had nothing to do with the end of our marriage. "

At the time of the separation, however, the news was so shocking as to lead to all kinds of speculation. Two of the more informed writers on the subject were "Suzy" the pseudonymous compiler of a society news column then in the New York *Daily News,* and Liz Smith, the *Daily News'* sage and shrewd chronciler of life in show business. "Sometimes," wrote "Suzy" on February 8, 1983, "their friends wonder how this whole Carson imbroglio came about. They feel that Joanna would like to remain Mrs. Johnny Carson, but Johnny would rather she didn't. Definitely didn't. He instigated the separation and now Joanna is just waiting for him to make an announcement of his plans . . . . No matter what you may have heard about both of them, the Carson split came as a surprise. At their tenth wedding anniversary several months ago, Johnny made an eloquent speech about what a wonderful, understanding wife Joanna was. He even flew her mother in for the party, and there wasn't a dry eye in the house."

Liz Smith reported the following startling news on January 27, 1983:

" . . . [The Carson separation] saddens friends of Johnny and Joanna. They remember only a few months ago when Johnny gave that surprise anniversary party for his wife at the same Beverly Hills Hotel suite where they honeymooned. At this party, Carson toasted his wife, praised her to the skies, and said how he'd be in terrible trouble without her. In the last year, Carson bought his wife two multimillion-dollar apartments—one in New York's Trump Tower for $3 million and another in the Pierre Hotel for $2 million after Joanna decided she'd prefer the convenience of room service, etc. Carson has always been super generous with his wife and today she owns a small valuable collection of top-drawer art as a result of his letting her say, 'Yes, I'll take that' and 'I'll take this' as she likes. Not long ago, Carson gifted Joanna with a piece of jewelry worth $250,000 in what some think was an effort to patch things up."

Johnny moved out of the St. Cloud Drive home in early November, taking up residence at the beach house in Malibu. At first, the two put on a brave and rather gallant front, while they continued to try to work things out, not only appearing at those dread charity events together, but also going to see Johnny's ailing father in Scottsdale, Arizona. "Johnny adored his father," Joanna says. "We were very involved as a family."

Nonetheless, it was a sad holiday season for both. "The breakup came just before Thanksgiving," recalls one of Joanna's friends, "and I know it was a very lonely time for her. She even had her secretary keep a bulletin board full of clips about Johnny.

It even included pictures of women he supposedly was going out with."

Joan Rivers told me at that time, "Johnny became deeply depressed. It was, after all, his third marriage, and I don't think either of them wanted it to end."

End it did though. "I think," says Richard Fischoff, "they might have patched it up, if they were different people in different circumstances. But I think things got away from them. It was very hard in the limelight . . . things got exaggerated and distorted. Soon it was a battle of the lawyers. They didn't have a chance."

"We communicated a lot by phone after the separation," Joanna recalls, "and we did see each other in person. Johnny was okay. [Just then, after the separation] we weren't even discussing the issues in a divorce. But there was a flurry of gossip in town. I mean we were still talking; he was calling me up to watch a certain movie on TV.

"I thought we could resolve anything. In the course of our marriage, we always used to talk about being able to resolve the big issues, whether it involved the children or the mother or the father, things that were really important . . . .

"We seemed to be able to resolve issues for much of the course of our marriage. We handled the decisions, the turnarounds in Johnny's career— 'Do you think I can ask for this, Babe? . . . Do you think that?'

"But then during the [1982] separation, when I thought we needed space from each other—that's why I asked him to go to our beach house—we ended up filing for divorce. I got a lot of calls from Johnny in the middle of the night then, negotiating with me.

"We'd talk and as we started delving into his world, so to speak, he was very agitated and very aggravated. I knew then I was dealing with two personalities—his, and Henry Bushkin's.

"You never knew who was really calling the shots and making the decisions. If Johnny had had a different kind of personality around him, advising him, who wasn't angrier than he was— Henry Bushkin, remember, was going through a sensational divorce at the time—I felt we could have resolved it . . . .

"Soon, Johnny was trying to negotiate the facts of the divorce with me on the phone—that if I would accept x, y, z, we could resolve the problem, and everything would be his. They were talking about money and property.

"They were going to offer me $15,000 a month, take it or leave it. I looked at my lawyers and said, 'I'll take my chances in court.' "

Joanna's attorneys filed papers which purported to show what her living expenses were. The documents alleged her life, based on an auditing of the family's books, cost $220,000 a month to maintain. Soon the newspapers were screaming that Joanna was asking for that much from Johnny.

"There was a campaign," says Joanna, "a deliberate campaign—not so much on Johnny's part—to have Johnny be the hero and have me be the gal who done him wrong. Deliberate, no question about it.

"All of a sudden these stories started to appear, and everyone starts asking me what about this $220,000 maintenance fee or whatever you want to call it. This was outrageous. Apparently, they took this number, and the press took this number, and said that's what I was asking for, when in fact that's not what I was asking for.

"I can only say I do know what I asked Johnny for in the presence of his lawyers and mine. They called him on the phone and told him the amount which I thought was a feasible amount to cover myself while we were going through these divorce proceedings.

"But he did not feel—and I never could figure out whether Johnny or Bushkin made the decision—it was right. They offered me $15,000—take it or leave it. That's when I told the lawyers to go to court."

The $2.6 million-a-year budget was printed in scores of papers. The glimpse it gave of the Carson house was fascinating. Among the numbers were expenditures of $37,065 a month for jewelry and furs; $12,625 a month for gifts to friends and relatives; $10,000 for maintenance fees on three New York City apartments; $3,955 a month for clothes; and $155 for flowers. Joanna's attorney, Arthur Crowley, said she was entitled to have temporary payments along those lines made to her because that "would enable her to maintain her status quo, her standard of living, until the divorce comes to trial."

Crowley also said the monthly $220,000 "is accurate to the penny as to what Mrs. Carson's living expenses were for 1982."

The vastness of these figures intrigued America and awakened Carson's own sense of humor. He went on camera and announced that his new hero in life had become Henry VIII, and said, "I heard from my cat's lawyer today. My cat wants $12,000 a month for Tender Vittles."

On another night he said, "An old lady stopped me on the street on my way to the show.

"She says, 'Johnny, I want a divorce from you.' And I say, 'But we're not even married.' She says, 'Yeah, but I want to skip right to the goodies.'

"I went to see my butcher the other day, Murray Giblets,"

he said another night. "I said, 'How do you pick a good turkey?' And he says, 'You ought to know. You're a three-time loser.' "

The jokes had an effect on Joanna. She stopped watching the show.

Although the judge allowed Joanna about $40,000 in temporary support, the $220,000 figure painted her as a mad spendthrift who required thousands of dollars a month for flowers and gifts. The joke around town was that if Joanna received the $220,000 a month, she'd use it to buy Nicaragua. She was subjected to severe ridicule for her request.

Joanna's friends, however, were entirely sympathetic to her demand. One put it this way:

"In Beverly Hills, the idea that eventually you'll be divorced is there right from the start. And unless you have a prenuptial agreement—and you'd be crazy to sign one of those—the first thing you do upon settling into your marriage is to arrange a budget for yourself that's as big and as expensive as you can manage.

"And it's a budget you expand, year after year after year, just like the Defense Department. You have to do this to make sure you get a fair shake in divorce court, because the alimony and support the judge gives you is based on what you spend. The more you spend the more you'll get.

"I don't regard it as money grubbing. It's payment for services. As a Beverly Hills housewife, you're a big part of your husband's career. You have to look spectacular all the time. You have to entertain lavishly. You have to keep up appearances around town. You should be paid for that. Not just in some allowance while you're married. You deserve, when the marriage breaks up, to be paid for all you did to make him the big shot he is when he leaves. "

As Jackie Collins, the author of *Hollywood Wives*, which allegedly contains elements of the Carson marriage, said, "You can always tell the Hollywood wives who are about to get divorced. You can find them in Fred's [the Rodeo Drive jeweler] stocking up like squirrels for the winter. " A salesman for Fred's told journalists that the Christmas before she and Johnny separated, Joanna came into the shop and picked out $100,000 worth of jewelry for herself, billing Johnny, of course, for the gifts.

Ellen Goodman, a nationally syndicated columnist, finally came to Joanna's defense. "The request for $2.6 million," wrote Ms. Goodman, "surely makes Joanna Carson a candidate for the hit parade of top ten spenders. Who can resist the temptation to award her the title of money-grubbing divorcee of the year. But . . . someone should present the other side . . . . If the Carsons were still married, we would regard her as no more than the overindulged wife of an overindulged performer . . . . Is it more outrageous for Joanna to be awarded $220,000 a month . . . than for Johnny to be paid $1.5 million a month by NBC?"

Joanna told reporters she was resigned to being regarded as the villainess of the piece because the American public "will forgive him [Johnny] anything.

"And, indeed, " she said, "they should. He comes to them at the most vulnerable time of their lives—when it's dark, when it's late, when they could be lonely or ill. They should forgive him because he makes them laugh. "

The court's final divorce order, issued on August 31, 1985, nearly three years after their separation, was no laughing matter. While Joanna received nothing like $2.6 million a year, she received a generous settlement in cash, real estate, and art.

"I asked the judge," Joanna says, "for what was fair and not a penny more. I felt just terrible at the way I was portrayed."

The eighty-page marriage dissolution document gave Joanna $2.24 million cash spread out in monthly payments until 1990, her death, or remarriage. She was also given the home on St. Cloud Drive in Bel-Air, privately estimated to be worth $8 million, along with three apartments in New York City, a 1976 Rolls Royce, a 1976 Mercedes Benz, a 1981 Datsun, 310 shares of stock in the Carson Broadcasting Corporation, and half of the remaining royalties on *The Tonight Show* paid between September 1972 and November 1982, when the court decreed the couple officially separated.

She also received some art work, including a Picasso.

Johnny, whose income in the divorce papers was estimated at $18 million a year, received their homes in Palm Springs and Las Vegas, an apartment in New York, a home in Scottsdale, Arizona, and, of course, the beach house in Malibu, along with two Mercedes, and the other half of the shares of the Carson Broadcasting Corporation, and half the payments for fees from *The Tonight Show* during the years of the marriage.

As Bob Newhart noted during an April 1985 dinner honoring Johnny for his support of a charity, "Johnny's greatest joy is finding new and talented young people and introducing them to fame and fortune. Unfortunately, most of them are his ex-wives."

And Johnny remarked, "My producer, Freddie de Cordova, really gave me something I need for Christmas. He gave me a gift certificate to the legal office of Jacoby & Myers."

It was an extremely rough time for Joanna who was portrayed, as Jody Wolcott Carson put it, "as a dragon lady, a horrible spendthrift."

195

Says one of her friends, "During and after the divorce, she became a virtual recluse—she didn't know who to trust, all these things were appearing in print about her! She was very hurt. She's holding her own in 1987."

Says another friend, Jan Sarnoff, "It annoys me when people call her materialistic. Heavens, Johnny makes almost $20 million a year—she's entitled to a fair share. And she's a real worker, an achiever, she's not your Chasen's-at-lunch-and-have-my-nails-done kind of woman. She had it hard after the divorce, but now she's going out with some fascinating men."

It was indeed a hard time. When Joanna, during the divorce, ran into Joan Rivers one day, she expressed the hope to Joan that they could still remain friends. Rivers told her no, candidly explaining that her relationship with Johnny was paramount, and she wouldn't risk it by befriending his ex-wife.

"Many of my friends just disappeared," says Joanna, "I find men are team players. They come together in a crisis. Women do not. That has to change.

"The experience of going through this marriage and divorce has taught me the value of honesty and communications in a relationship. I love this present generation—they are so open and honest and supportive of each other.

"At one time, we were all in the lawyers' office getting ready for the divorce. Johnny was there too. I turned to him and said, 'You know this is just dumb.' And he said to me—he may even have been undecided then—'Yes, but I guess it's the thing to do.' "

During their last meeting, when all the final legal work had been done, Johnny turned to Joanna, after signing their divorce papers, and said, "What I'll miss the most, is not being able to talk to you."

The pain of the divorce for Johnny was real, and severe. This was, after all, his third marriage. But the divorce also meant an end to the suffocation and stultification of the Beverly Hills lifestyle. As Fred de Cordova once said, "Johnny doesn't need to go to other cocktail parties. *The Tonight Show* is his cocktail party. That's where he sparkles."

The show once again would be the most important thing in his life. "Johnny's wives are part of his act," says first wife, Jody Wolcott Carson.

He may not be entirely happy about that.

"My giving advice about marriage," he has said, "is like the captain of the Titanic giving instructions on navigation." Though he is smiling, there is some sorrow in that joke.

15
Joanna Speaks

T he divorce of Johnny and Joanna Carson is one of the most celebrated in recent American history. Johnny often mentioned it on his show, and the press covered it closely, paying special attention to the huge sums of money involved. But the entire episode was seen mostly from Johnny's perspective, which he often expressed in the monologue. Joanna Carson, until now, has never spoken at length about her life with Johnny. Here Joanna tells her side of the story, while giving us a picture of their highly private life together in the midst of Bel-Air and Beverly Hills. Portions of Joanna's remarks are also excerpted in other chapters of this book.

Q: Wasn't it mostly a good marriage, though?

"Oh it sure was a good marriage for the most part. After we were married on September 30, 1972, which was the tenth anniversary of *The Tonight Show*—that was part of the excitement—we bought the house on St. Cloud Drive in Bel-Air. We bought it from Kitty and Mervyn LeRoy, who built the house. [A prominent movie producer and director, LeRoy directed, among other films, *The Wizard of Oz*.] I had a decorator come from New York, and he pulled the best from my apartment and Johnny's apartment, and we had a very pretty house, warm, people loved to come to it.

"We did not do too much entertaining, though. Johnny works every day, so by the time we got home, we preferred to have dinner with each other, with my son, with family . . . I had my activities in the day, and I enjoyed, most of the time, staying at home. I had to create an atmosphere for us. Once I create an atmopshere, I loved to have people in our atmosphere, as did Johnny. So we got along very well on that level.

"I liked introducing Johnny to travel too. He had never been to Italy or to France, until we were married. I think one time, in the sixties, he was in London for two nights for a show. That was as far as his travelling went.

"Our first trip to Europe was probably in 1974. We started to go to the south of France, and Johnny became very interested in tennis. That also started when we moved to California. And we used to go to Wimbledon, in London, for the tennis matches every year, and then travel to the south of France before coming home.

"I don't know that Johnny really loved travelling. He has a natural curiosity like a man of his stature does, but Johnny is also very American—he likes to know what drawer his socks are in. It's all very basic.

"The interesting thing for me was that he wasn't known in Europe, so I could walk with him anyplace I wanted to—walk like a normal person, eating an ice cream cone, and not have people around us. The Europeans knew Johnny's name, and they knew it was a famous name, but they didn't bother us very much, so it was time together that was very meaningful to me, and I really cherished it.

"One year I promised him I was going to take him to Italy, and we went. It was in 1980 and we had a wonderful time. We flew to Rome and did all the things that people do in Rome for the first time—we saw the Vatican and went to the Borghese Gardens and ate pasta and drank wonderful wine and sat in the plazas. And then we drove from Rome to Ravello, and we stayed with Gore Vidal and Howard Austin in Ravello. Then we went to Capri on the hydrofoil—and that was something I always wanted to do with Johnny. It was a very special time for me because I never thought I'd get him there. And I remember that we got off the hydrofoil and looked at the funicular railway that goes up the side of the mountain, and he couldn't believe what was going on and I said to him, 'I got you here, and I'm so happy.' "

Q: When did things change?

"Johnny is a very complex personality, and the pressure on him is great. I feel around 1980 I started to surmise some of the things that were going wrong with the marriage . . . ."

Q: Were other women, as had often been rumored, a problem?

"When you are married to someone like Johnny and the women of today, who perhaps weren't as highly principled as I am . . . well, that goes with the territory, and there were certainly times when you just look away. There are times when you just say, 'Well, my commitment is to my family and my investment in a relationship with my emotions and my giving . . . . ' Well, I thought everything would take care of itself.

"All the women that I respect who have gone through similar experiences tend to feel you should look away, and if the family is strong and basically unfragmented, it will hold together. I'm a highly principled lady, and I [was] very involved with family—Johnny, Johnny's family, his mother, his father, his children, his brother, his sister—were important to me. They were my priorities, right there with my own family—my mother, my brother, and my son. Johnny's family was very important to me. I used to find myself bringing them all together . . . .

"Johnny adored his father. And when, in the early eighties, his father and mother couldn't make up their minds about where to spend their winter months, I went to Scottsdale and met with them week after week, to help them, to guide them. They finally bought a house in Scottsdale, and I went up and decorated it with all my furniture from my Fifth Avenue apartment.

"I felt that my role was to get them together. Johnny found it a burden to be so concentrated on a career and 'making it', so I felt *my* role was to bring the family together for him, for the holidays . . . .I'd say, 'Okay, you're all going to be here for Thanksgiving . . . you're all coming for Christmas' or 'It's Father's Day and your father has just done the most magnificent performance on the Academy Awards, and nobody has called him up to say how great he was! I don't understand that!' I'd talk to the family on that level.

"I remember particularly Jody [Carson, Johnny's first wife and the mother of his three children] called me one evening, out of a clear blue sky, and she thanked me! She kept me on the phone a long time, thanking me. I said, 'Jody, for what? Why are you thanking me?'

"She said, 'I'm thanking you because you're giving my boys back to me.' I thought that was a very interesting remark, because I always told the boys they had to be concerned about their mother, they must be concerned about their mother, what she was doing and so forth.

"I think [they did] not see her as often as [they] should have, but then this strong, principled person was saying to them, 'You must care for your mother . . . you must call her on the holidays—it's Mother's Day . . . .'

"But around 1980, I began to notice changes."

Q: Can you say what the problems were?

"No comment. No. I was the one who was supposed to be the yelling, screaming Italian who would lose her temper, and the bottom line is that it was the reverse. Sometimes, I was scared. I told him I was scared because sometimes when he drank, he was a totally different personality. There were times I was scared. And he does have a temper, flies off the handle. He has a very difficult time saying he's sorry.

"He wasn't like that from the beginning. Or at least it was something that I didn't see. I would say that in late 1980 I started to see a definite change . . . . Something that I didn't understand.

"Johnny would discuss the issues, the problems. We just couldn't resolve them. I used to say to him, 'If you would devote as much time to our relationship, our marriage, to your family, as you devote to that show, you couldn't help but have a "hit" on your hands.'

"It was very difficult for me to have a husband, and I think for the children to have a father, whom everybody emulated and loved and related to, and then when you saw the reverse side, you just wanted to say, 'Why? Why is that which everybody in

203

the nation loves and gets, not there for me? Why was it not there for his children, his family, certainly his mother?'

"So you ask yourself, 'Am I asking too much from a human being? Is this not something he can handle?'

"It was a very good marriage for most of the time. He used to talk about it on the show all the time— 'This was it.' But we just couldn't resolve the problems that arose. I think we tried for a year and a half, and ultimately I didn't want to lose respect for myself and wake up in the morning and not like me, because I like me a lot.

"We went to an analyst together. It helped in the sense that maybe it brought things to the surface, but you can't go to an analyst and not tell the truth. And when I was around, he didn't tell the truth. I don't know what he did privately. I think somewhere along the way, you try so hard, you try to resolve things when . . . . I just kind of lost respect for him.

"I think that's what happened to me.

"So I made the decision that this marriage was not going anywhere, was not continuing in the manner it should, especially with all the time put into it! So I asked Johnny to leave the house, to go to our beach house and stay there. I think there was a certain shock, a certain anger—it hurts the male ego—and that's when the stories started that the whole thing was about money. That's when the press started perceiving me as greedy, as going after the pockets of the man that I loved. That was outrageous. Money was never even a subject that came up in our marriage. It hurt me badly; money had nothing to do with the end of our marriage. "

Q: Did you talk after your separation?

"We communicated a lot by phone after the separation, and we did see each other in person. Johnny was okay. [Just then, after the separation] we weren't even discussing the issues in a divorce. But there was a flurry of gossip in town. I mean we were still talking; he was calling me up to watch a certain movie on TV.

"I thought we could resolve anything. In the course of our marriage, we always used to talk about being able to resolve the big issues, whether it involved the children or the mother or the father, things that were really important.

"In 1972, we separated for a couple of months. It really wasn't serious, and we knew we could work it out. I just felt then I needed space. I was new in the community, and I needed some adjustment period. Nobody knew. Not even one person on *The Tonight Show*. We decided we wouldn't tell anybody. And we didn't. All you have to do is tell one person in this town, and forget it! Everybody knows! We also agreed that we would not be seeing anyone else while we were separated. We missed each other very much. And we worked it out.

"We seemed to be able to resolve issues for much of the course of our marriage. We handled the decisions, the turnarounds in Johnny's career—'Do you think I can ask for this, Babe? . . . Do you think that?'

"But then during the [1982] separation, when I thought we needed space from each other—that's why I asked him to go to our beach house—we ended up filing for divorce. I got a lot of calls from Johnny in the middle of the night then, negotiating with me.

"We'd talk and as we started delving into his world, so to speak, he was very agitated and very aggravated. I knew then I was dealing with two personalities—his, and Henry Bushkin's [Johnny Carson's attorney].

"You never knew who was really calling the shots and making

the decisions. If Johnny had had a different kind of personality around him, advising him, who wasn't angrier than he was—Henry Bushkin, remember, was going through a sensational divorce at the time—I felt we could have resolved it.

"If I would tell Johnny what I considered to be the facts of our life—not necessarily personal facts, but other facts—he had Mr. Bushkin to tell him I was wrong . . . that I was scheming.

"Soon, Johnny was trying to negotiate the facts of the divorce with me on the phone—that if I would accept x, y, z, we could resolve the problem and everything would be his. They were talking about money and property.

"There was a campaign, a deliberate campaign—not so much on Johnny's part—to have Johnny be the hero and have me be the gal who done him wrong. Deliberate, no question about it.

"All of a sudden these stories started to appear, and everyone starts asking me what about this $220,000 maintenance fee or whatever you want to call it. This was outrageous. Apparently, they took this number, and the press took this number, and said that's what I was asking for, when in fact that's not what I was asking for.

"I can only say I do know what I asked Johnny for in the presence of his lawyers and mine. They called him on the phone and told him the amount which I thought was a feasible amount to cover myself while we were going through these divorce proceedings.

"But he did not feel—and I never could figure out whether Johnny or Bushkin made the decision—it was right. They offered me $15,000 [a month]—take it or leave it. That's when I told the lawyers to file, that I'd take my chances in court.

"I asked the judge for what was fair and not a penny more. I felt just terrible at the way I was portrayed."

Q: Johnny frequently made jokes about your divorce on the show. How did you feel about them?

"When I tell you that from the moment I filed for divorce, I never watched the show again, I hope you believe me. It was simply too painful. Today I won't watch the show even. Obviously, every performance was taped by my lawyers and I would hear about the jokes . . . . There was no way to shut him up.

"He has that forum, *The Tonight Show*, every single night to tell whatever he wants to, to paint the facts however he wants. He sometimes uses that show like it was an analyst's couch. He just kind of says those things, and everyone applauds, and they think it's very funny.

"I was shocked by the jokes, but knowing Johnny as well as I did, well . . . when Johnny's in a lot of pain like most comedians, they revert to their humorous side and they cover up the pain that way. They learn to do that when they are little children. When they're having a confrontation with their mommy, all they want to do is to get mommy to love them, to make mommy laugh.

"When I heard about these jokes, I knew he was in a lot of pain because I saw him go through this before—with children, with family, with other performers he had a hate-on for . . . and he'd just attack them on the show because he was in pain over it. Most comedians do that. Sometimes I laughed; I thought it was funny. Other times, I wanted to say, 'Stop it, Johnny. You're getting a lot of mileage on this thing, and it's simply not funny.'

"Sometimes, he'd have the writers come in, and we'd listen to the jokes they were suggesting he might do, and after one joke, I recall, I just said, 'You know, that's tasteless.' And Johnny turned to the writers and said, 'If she says it's tasteless, it's tasteless.' And they'd delete it. And when I watched the Academy

207

Awards, after we were separated, and Johnny did one joke that the audience booed. And I said to myself, 'Oh Johnny, you didn't have anybody to edit for you—that was really tasteless.' "

Q: What other effects did you feel?

"Many of my friends just disappeared. I find men are team players. They come together in a crisis. Women do not. That has to change.

"What I went through was just uncivilized. At times it broke me down mentally, emotionally, and physically. But it could never reach my spirit, because my spirit said, 'I am going to fight because I know I'm right.' But it was an awful experience. For my family as well. My mother was very upset. She adored Johnny.

"For a year and a half after the divorce, I was healing. It's like a death in the family, and you have to come to grips with what you're going to do with your own life. I was in a very secluded world, and had to go through a weeding out. There's nothing like what I went through to show you who your friends are. Actually, that was a blessing in disguise. I'm still involved in the same charities, and I've had some interesting other offers.

"For about a year and a half after my divorce from Johnny, I was really torn about where I wanted to live. That's sort of an interesting time for women when you go through what I went through. All of a sudden, you have to guide your own destiny. You're on your own, and that's something that lawyers and the divorce and the courts never prepare you for."

Q: You were involved in a business with dress designer Michael Volbracht. How did the divorce effect that?

"In 1980, I decided I needed a new challenge. Being Johnny's wife was wonderful, but living in this kind of community was almost like fantasy. It wasn't realistic, and somewhere along the line you get out of touch with your own feelings about what you really want to do. So on one trip to New York, when I was visiting my mom, a girlfriend of mine told me about a designer, Michael Volbracht.

"I'm very interested in art, and what attracted me to Volbracht was that he worked so unusually. He painted portraits or fantasies or flowers and then put them on silk, and out of the fabric he would design dresses. I thought to myself, here is a young, talented designer. I thought I could handle getting a dress business going. It was a real challenge, but I thought I could handle it all.

"I'm not really someone who likes to sit and have lunch with the ladies. I like to be doing things and thought this would be interesting. I thought I could handle it all.

"I think a lot of the divorce proceedings got in the way of the business. I was so fragmented that I couldn't make decisions to protect myself here, and be involved in New York.

"As a matter of fact, when I went to shows to see collections, I just felt embarrassed. I couldn't handle it all emotionally. I would sit at a collection and be wondering what was going through everyone's head. I wasn't focussed. I just couldn't be at that time.

"So therefore, I think the divorce proceedings seemed to work against us. People were believing what they were reading, and they didn't think I was taking it seriously when, in fact, I was. I don't like to lose money, that's one thing about me. And this turned out to be a big financial failure for me. Also as a female it was a failure in the sense that I found a challenge and I didn't see it through. We dissolved the partnership not long ago."

Q: What are your own plans now?

"Ultimately, I will do something that involves a meaningful project that will help other women. Because during a divorce like mine, you recognize that when that little lady in Kansas with two kids who has to work day and night and has to fight to get support, well, her pain is the same as mine. Her anxieties are the same as mine were.

"My settlement from the court may have had a lot of zeros at the end of the numbers, many more perhaps than hers, but all the feelings, all the trauma, and all the crazy times you go through when you're getting a divorce—they're the same. The lady in Kansas is up against the same system, the same legal system, lawyers, and bills. It was just that mine was bigger and more expensive. But the basic feelings and stress that divorce brings into your life are exactly the same."

Q: Will you marry again?

"Probably. I like to be in a relationship. The kind of man who interests me would be someone who would allow me space. I'm very spiritual, and I'd like somebody who views the world through his heart as well as his head."

Q: How do you feel about Johnny's upcoming marriage to Alexis Mass? What do you think about her?

"I haven't met her. I don't know her. I don't know if Johnny will succeed in his new marriage. He's tried Jody, Joanne, and Joanna. But he might just get it right this time; he's older now. Perhaps he has learned something about anger. I wish him well."

16
In the Groove

Despite the turmoil in his private life, Johnny had, by the early eighties, become truly unbeatable. As Ed McMahon, his trusty sidekick, once said, "Every day, no matter what is going on in his life, he has to come out there and *be* Johnny Carson." And after twenty years of doing just this, Johnny had so defined America's idea of what late-night television ought to be, that his competition was failing before starting. But, television being an industry built on wild dreams, late-night alternatives to *The Tonight Show* kept being proffered. One of them came from an old antagonist, Fred Silverman.

Silverman, who was the NBC president whose insensitive handling of Carson had helped bring Johnny to the brink of resignation in 1979, had himself resigned from the presidency of NBC in 1981. His replacement was Grant Tinker, the former husband of Mary Tyler Moore and the former head of the independent production company which produced not only her show but other hits like *The Bob Newhart Show, Rhoda,* and *Remington Steele.* And as Tinker became a network head, Silverman established himself in independent production.

Soon thereafter he had an idea for a new show, which suggested he still believed Johnny wasn't doing things right. Silverman managed to syndicate, that is, to sell to independent or non-network-affiliated stations, a new late-night talk show to compete against Carson. The host of the new show was Alan Thicke, a young Canadian whose afternoon talk show had garnered that country's best audience ratings. Thicke had also been a writer for American television, with credits for *Fernwood 2night,* a wickedly funny satire on soap operas, and its successor, *America 2Night*, a hilarious parody of bad talk shows.

Described as a "jack-of-all-trades"—a not auspicious cliche—Thicke was, in fact, funny personally and was a good interviewer and a decent musician. Unfortunately, he didn't have much of a chance to use these talents on his show, which never got off the ground. From the outset there was panic on the set. To compensate for bland guests and interviews that had viewers turning dials, the producers tried increasing the show's pace, but instead of quick, lively entertainment, they got what to many was simply bewildering confusion. *Thicke of the Night* turned out to be an unintentional parody of a talk show. And while the *America 2Night* parody had been clever, *Thicke of the Night* was inept. The embarrassing enterprise wobbled on for a year before stumbling into talk-show oblivion, where it joined other

Carson competitors like *The Joey Bishop Show, The Mike Douglas Show, The Dick Cavett Show,* and *The David Frost Show.*

Even though *The Tonight Show* had absolute dominance in its time spot in the United States, and even though Americans obviously loved Johnny Carson whether his life was neat or on the rocks, foreigners found the occasional foray of *The Tonight Show* into their climes anything but tonic. In hindsight, it's simply remarkable Johnny and his staff thought a show so topical, and so American, could translate overseas. But such was the "can-do" spirit of *The Tonight Show* and its staff in the early eighties that they thought they could air the show successfully abroad. For a few months, from autumn 1981 into 1982, an abbreviated version of *The Tonight Show* was shown in Great Britain. Usually, one of the previous week's shows was cut to forty minutes and sent over. The British almost sent them back.

"Seventy percent of the jokes mean Sweet Fanny Adams to us up here," said a spokesman for a Scottish network, which very briefly broadcast the show.

"Maybe subtitles would help, or footnotes," reported *Time* magazine. "Carson's opening monologue, with its repeated references to daily U.S. political folkways and wild consumerism may be delivered in what is roughly considered a common language, but the jokes turn out to be not fully translatable."

"His monologue could be in Swahili for all we get from it," wrote one Joe Steeples in London's *Daily Mail.*

The editor of the British humor magazine *Punch* really took after *The Tonight Show* in our own *TV Guide.*

"Johnny Carson," wrote *Punch's* Alan Coren, "had been heavily pre-marketed to us as a unique television performer, in that he was both brilliant comic and scintillating conversationalist: some extraordinary amalgam of Sid Caesar and Gore Vidal, or

Mel Brooks and Bill Buckley, Jr., or George Burns and Oliver Wendell Holmes. Not surprisingly, our appetites were whetted to a razor's edge, our tubeside seats drawn in an eager ring, for the first, fine, careless rapture.

"And then a small man in a sharp suit came on, read bad gags off an unseen idiot board and laughed at them himself, for no good reason. After that, a marmoset sat on his head and peed down his collar. This went on for a while, and then it was time to go and watch an aardvark foul its sandbox."

Of course, the Brits were probably expecting something on a truly high plane—like Benny Hill. This slight blow to Johnny's ego was eased by the fact that *The Tonight Show* in America was nearing its twentieth anniversary. There were some odd celebrations of this fact, including the naming of a medical disorder.

The distinguished *New England Journal of Medicine,* in January 1982, reported the discovery of a disorder which it called *Carsongenous monocular nyctalopia,* or Johnny Carson night blindness. A Dr. J. Park Biehl reported the discovery. The problem came to the attention of the Cincinnati doctor when a thirty-year-old female patient complained of blindness in her left eye at night. According to the *Journal,* "She noticed the problem after turning off the television in her bedroom." The doctor questioned her some more, and discovered that the problem came from watching television while lying down in bed with her head turned sideways on a pillow. In that position, "her right eye was buried in the pillow, while she watched Johnny Carson with her left. Naturally, when it came time to turn off the set, she could see well only with the dark-adapted right eye."

Given all the things that have taken place in bedrooms while people watch Johnny Carson (There have been reports of couples

214

who find the monologue integral to intimate activities), this was a first: an actual disorder named for Johnny.

And even though Johnny had become a superstar among superstars, with the country's largest nightly audiences, he continued, in the early eighties, to perform with great success in Las Vegas. Johnny's two-hour show was usually opened by a singer of the Phyllis McGuire class: brassy, loud, and definitely a performer. Near the end of the first hour, Johnny himself would appear to the howling of the crowd. He would do a racier version of his monologue and then settle into a series of skits that hilariously but unselfconsciously followed the adventures of a young Johnny Carson in the rural Midwest. Most of the material dealt with how he came of age sexually: first dates; the fear of growing blind from shunned practices; first dates with soft touches; and of course, the trip to the drugstore to buy condoms. As late as the early eighties, the word *condom*, now spoken everywhere, was risqué, even in a casino.

His show included parodies of current trends, including one on condominiums for the dead, which was built around a character who was a wicked combination of a nasty cemetery salesman and a huckstering real estate promoter. And invariably he closed with his famous skit about Deputy John, the kiddie show host on TV, who has to suffer the little children through the world's most dreadful hangover. Deputy John, who harkens back to the early days on WOW, was one of Johnny's favorite characters. Indeed, the concert shows, over the years, grew increasingly concerned with Johnny's youth.

His roots, especially in light of his divorces and the aging and death of his parents, had caused him, in Johnny's own phrase, "to hearken back to my youth on the plains." (Johnny's father, Homer Carson, died in April 1983. His mother, Ruth Carson,

215

died in October 1985. Both were in their eighties at the time of their deaths.)

In 1982, NBC broadcast a special built around Johnny's return to Norfolk, Nebraska, for a reunion with the Norfolk High School Class of 1943. On the evening of the reunion dinner, Johnny spoke to his classmates:

"I think there's a great advantage to grow up in a community where you feel comfortable. Hell, I remember never having to lock the doors when I was living back here. Kids would come in day or night. There was a closeness that we all miss, I am sure." He broke away from his serious tone, to speak about matters usually reserved for his concert show.

"As in all small towns, there are certain 'nice' girls, girls that you marry—and girls that you do not. Well, there was this girl, I'll call her Francine, and Francine, well, 'put out'—at least that's what was going around. I finally got up enough nerve to ask her out, she said yes, and you can imagine my excitement . . . Mount Vesuvius! But then I had to overcome a problem—protection. I went up to the drugstore counter and the druggist yelled, 'Well, John, what can I do for you?' Luckily, then he saw that I had Francine waiting in the car, and he knowingly handed over the goods. I remember I had, as we used to put it, a 'swell' time."

Going home seemed to have awakened in him a sense of what really made him tick. He was in touch with his past again and headed for a simpler life, away from the black-tie circuit of Beverly Hills. He also, after his third divorce, had a new lady in his life. Johnny was moving from one groove to another.

17
The New Mrs. Carson

T he new woman in Johnny Carson's life, the woman who became his fourth wife on June 20, 1987, in a ceremony at Johnny's home attended by just the marrying judge and Johnny's brother Dick, is a mystery who suddenly appeared out of nowhere in 1984, when she became the woman on Johnny's arm. She is a stunning blonde, but was a complete unknown.

Her name was believed to be Alex "Maas," but her mystery deepened when, for the purposes of this book, we went in search of Alex's history and were startled to find that the state of California had not one single document, or shred of information, about an Alex "Maas." There was no driver's license, motor vehicle registration, or voter's registration. But the dazzling Alex was all too real.

"She's even more sleek and sophisticated than she was when she first met Johnny a few years ago," says a Carson colleague who is in daily contact with him. "I guess it was hard at first being Johnny Carson's girlfriend, but she's really grown into it. I said to her the other day, 'You know you are *so* beautiful, it hurts to look at you.'

"All I really know about her is that she's not in show business, has no desire to be in show business, but she has a sharp mind for stocks and bonds. She used to work for a couple of bank presidents. But she doesn't work now. She's Johnny's girlfriend, full time."

Friends of Johnny insist the two are ideally suited for one another. "I think Alexis is very good for Johnny," says the wife of one Carson executive. "She gives him a center and focus and doesn't need to be a separate personality or star. Alexis is contented to be a consort. Joanna wanted to be a star in her own right."

Another friend characterizes her as "not ambitious, not tough talking, and relatively unworldly. She looks far more stylish now than when they met . . . almost sophisticated."

Johnny's second wife, Joanne, likes Alex (or Alexis, as the Hollywood crowd has named her). "I think Alexis is a super lady, and she's great for him. He was very social there for a while with his third wife. Now he seems to have reverted back to a simpler lifestyle, and Alexis is suited for that."

"Whether Johnny permits [her personal growth] or not is another story," says a man about town who has known Carson since the sixties. "Alex is definitely developing. She has a new presence, a new stylishness, and a look that says, hey, I'm really comfortable being Johnny Carson's girlfriend."

She also has a new apartment—worth about $450,000—that Johnny has provided. It serves them both as an in-town home when they are not at the beach, which is where Johnny met Alexis.

According to the widely believed story, Johnny first saw Alexis walking on the beach in front of his home. Neighbors have said the meeting was more than chance; that Alexis, who did not live nearby, frequently strolled in front of the Carson cabana. At any rate, they were soon dating, and photographers who were used to seeing Johnny with Sally Fields, Angel Tompkins, Angie Dickinson, Loni Anderson and scores of others, found themselves wondering who the new lady was. She was identified to them as Alex, or Alexis, or Alexandra "Maas."

It's a sign of Johnny's contempt for the press that he and Alexis have let all these years go by without bothering to tell the press they've been misspelling the name of Johnny's girlfriend. Her real name is Alexandra Mass, and under that name the state of California's documents files provide much information. She was born, the files reveal, on April 9, 1950. She has blonde hair and blue eyes, is five feet seven inches tall and weighs 119 pounds.

One friend of Johnny's who does know her background told us, "Alexis is great, a real nice Catholic girl—though she attends church only sporadically. I've met her family. Her father is a travelling salesman, she has a younger sister, and her mother is a housewife.

"Her parents are nice, middle class people and are very good looking. Alexis was born and grew up in Pittsburgh, and went to Mount Mercy Catholic School in Pennsylvania. She majored in art history and is very interested in art. So is Johnny, of course;

219

it's one of the things they have in common. His tastes are very eclectic, but in art he's interested strictly in Contemporary art.

"He's interested in everything—from astronomy to the space program to flying. It was Joanna who introduced him to Europe, which he loves because people don't recognize him there. And he's been back several times with Alex—especially to tennis tournaments. They travel a lot together. They go to San Francisco often. Alex is a good friend to Johnny. This will be her first marriage. She never married before because she never found the right man. She really loves Johnny, and he really loves her."

After finishing her education, Alexis moved, not to Los Angeles, but to Boston, where she became involved in that city's local glamour industry: politics.

From 1975 to 1979 she worked as the administrative assistant to a top official in the Massachusetts State House, David Liederman, who himself was Governor Michael Dukakis' chief secretary. She shared a Beacon Hill apartment for a while with Pat Mitchell, a woman who was a leading Boston television personality.

Alex's former boss recalls, "She came in with a good resume and clearly was a lovely person. She had, in fact, movie-star quality. She worked out to be a perfect administrator—she would answer the phones and trouble-shoot for the governor. She had good skills and was great with people. She'd never get annoyed. She and Pat Mitchell were always going to events . . . . In fact, she was already travelling in the world of celebrities.

"She dated a little as I recall, but very selectively. She was always talking about going out to California for a vacation. I had a feeling about that. I told her, 'If you go out to California, you'll never come back.' That's exactly what happened. She did go out to California and fell in love with it. About a month after she returned, she announced she was moving there.

"I visited L.A. a few years later, in the spring of 1982, and we had lunch in Westwood. She hadn't met Johnny yet, but she was having a great time. She had an apartment in Westwood, near the UCLA campus, and was working for the chairman of one of the big department stores there as his personal assistant. She had also worked for the presidents of two banks. I recall she said she went horseback riding a lot and liked eating at good restaurants."

Dolores Mitchell, who is now president of the Katherine Gibbs School in Boston, worked with Alexis at the State House. She remembers Alexis as "pleasant, friendly and a good worker . . . one of three or four young women in the front office who fielded the enormous number of phone calls the governor received.

"Alexis was stunning looking . . . . She had a kind of Farrah Fawcett look with her mane of hair . . . and she clearly had an active social life . . . . She'd go tootling off to New York for weekends leaving us plebian folk on the sidelines saying, Wow!"

Westwood—the area of Los Angeles to which Alexis moved when she came to California—is the same neighborhood in which she lives now, albeit in very different circumstances. Westwood, which is just south of Bel-Air and west of Beverly Hills, is an extensive neighborhood of single family homes, small apartment houses, and some very large new high-rises. It was built as a development surrounding the new University of California at Los Angeles in the late twenties, and is still a favorite—though a high-priced favorite—neighborhood for academics, students, and young singles looking for an urban, rather than suburban, environment. Alexis lived in a smaller, older apartment house within hailing distance of a stretch of Wilshire Boulevard now called the Wilshire Gulch, which is where she currently lives.

The Gulch is a half-mile stretch of Wilshire Boulevard lined with high-rise apartment buildings, handsome and gaudy. These buildings, constructed in the last ten years or so, were part of the incredible real estate boom that hit Los Angeles in the mid-seventies. While celebrities abound in these crannies, the area was overbuilt, and few of the buildings are fully occupied. Nevertheless, the neighborhood is a classy one.

A movie producer who met Alexis in the early eighties recalls that then she seemed interested in making the move from her small Westwood apartment to one of the condominiums in the Gulch. He also remembers Alexis as "sweet" and "selective"— especially about dating.

"Although," recalls the producer, "Alexis was and is younger than I was and, of course, am, I had the odd sense in the back of my mind that she thought I was too young for her. Too young, and not well established enough in the industry, and not wealthy enough. Not to say that she's a fortune hunter. I just had the idea that in dating she was holding out for someone who could do more for her than I possibly could. And I think she found it in Johnny."

She now has made the move from her small apartment in Westwood to a handsome apartment in the Wilshire Gulch. After two years of dating, Johnny bought Alex her spectacular Wilshire Boulevard apartment in a building which describes itself in advertisements in *The New Yorker* and elsewhere as "the most exclusive address in America." One of her neighbors is Tom Selleck.

"Her apartment is one of the prettiest," says a building staff member. "It's a two-bedroom, two-and-one-half-bath on a high floor, facing south with a full, dramatic view of Los Angeles and the ocean."

Extrapolating from price charts, it would appear that Johnny paid about $450,000 for the apartment, which includes membership in a health club, complete with swimming pool and Jacuzzi. The building's lobby, all in white marble, is tall, wide and spacious and is furnished with antique furniture and pale, pastel Persian rugs.

"Alexis' apartment," says a friend of Johnny, "is very pretty. It's not the most deluxe apartment in the building, but it could have been.

"When they decided to take an apartment together," he explained, "Alexis went in and looked and asked if they could rent. The building managers at first said no, that the apartments were strictly for sale, not for rent. But finally they said yes because the building, in fact, was nearly empty, and it really wouldn't hurt to have additional tenants making it look lively.

"They showed her an apartment on the first floor. She liked it and said, 'I'll bring my boyfriend back on Sunday to look at it.' And that Sunday she walks in with Johnny Carson!

"The first thing he said on seeing the apartment was 'not high enough.' So they showed them an apartment higher up. Johnny rented it for a few months, and then they bought it. The point is the agents could have shown them the penthouse, which was vacant then—it sold for $2 million. They'd probably have taken it."

Friends report that Johnny, not Alex, supervised the decorating, choosing dove gray and taupes with black accents giving the apartment "a soft, classic, but contemporary design."

"This apartment is much dressier than the beach house," one

guest reports, "and Alexis makes a great hostess on those few occasions when they entertain."

Johnny and Alex don't socialize very much now. Says Freddie de Cordova, Johnny's producer, "Johnny has done his share of Friars roasts, no more of those. And he only does a minimum of charities now—only those he can identify with in some way. He emceed the recent Jimmy Stewart charity special on TV, but that's because he's real fond of Jimmy."

After the day's taping, he and Alexis eschew the social circuit for dinner with friends. Henry "Bombastic" Bushkin, despite all the ups and downs of their business enterprises, remains his closest friend. He plays poker occasionally on Friday nights with show-business pals like Chevy Chase, who has become a close friend, Steve Martin, and a couple of movie industry executives. A newer friend is Marvin Davis, the oil billionaire who once owned the 20th Century-Fox movie studios and company, and who now owns the Beverly Hills Hotel.

Typically, following a taping, you can find Johnny and Alexis and Mr. and Mrs. Marvin Davis dining at a place like Morton's in West Hollywood. (Since the Beverly Hills City Council in March 1987 banned smoking in restaurants, Johnny and his Pall Malls often head outside the city limits. The ban, incidentally, prompted a flurry of monologue jokes such as, "I understand the Beverly Hills City Council has banned sex in restaurants because it might lead to smoking afterwards.")

He usually eats a hamburger, or swordfish, and french fries. "Alex eats whatever Johnny eats," says a waiter, "or fish and a plain green salad. She's very skinny. He doesn't drink, and usually they have no dessert." Other favorite dining spots include Spago in West Hollywood, La Famiglia in Beverly Hills, or La Scala in Malibu. Sometimes Johnny will stop at Coop's in

Brentwood, a neighborhood between Westwood and the beach, on his way home.

"Mostly," says Johnny, "I go right home after the taping." In his new life, socializing is at a minimum. He spends his time with Alex and just a few other people. Says John McMahon, a former Carson executive and now head of United Artists, "Johnny now has just a small circle of friends and leads a relatively simple life."

For that life, Alex seems ideal. She likes art, astronomy, travel, and the homelife. Her lack of interest in socializing means that Johnny has much more time and energy for his first love: *The Tonight Show*. Not surprisingly, shortly after Johnny's engagement to Alex Mass was announced, he also announced that he had signed a new contract with NBC, which extended his tenure three years beyond the twenty-fifth anniversary of *The Tonight Show*. He's come a long way from the days in Beverly Hills that saw him tired, if not exhausted, and ready to quit.

"I'm in my groove now," he's said about his new life— mornings in Malibu, afternoons in Burbank, and easy evenings away from the crowd.

But what is the special appeal of Alex? Why Alex? In addition to their apparent compatability, Jody Carson, Johnny's first wife, offers this thought: "When I first met John, he was dating a sorority sister, a beauty queen whose name, ironically enough, was Marge Alexis. I often think it's funny that Johnny had to go through Joan (my real name is Joan, not Jody), Joanne, and Joanna to get back to Alexis."

18
Shining Hour

I t is now 5:29 p.m., Los Angeles time, but here in Studio One of the NBC Studios in Burbank, the clocks read 11:29. Ed McMahon, Doc Severinsen, and Fred de Cordova each have spent a few minutes in the last half hour getting the audience in the mood for the show. The jokes are the same ones they tell night after night. Nonetheless, they unload the goofy old groaners with vigor, humor, and enthusiasm.

The band members, zany and lively, are in their spots, instruments at the ready. Ed McMahon, holding some notes with the names of tonight's guests typed on them, stands in front of his microphone, just to the left of *The Tonight Show* couch.

His smile is eager, his throat is clear, he is now ready once again to introduce the man he's worked with for thirty-one years.

The pros are, indeed, ready. But it's the audience that is thrilled with excitement. They are really ready: There's the smiling grandmother in tweeds, who is the library chairman back home in Carroll County, New Hampshire. She's in Los Angeles visiting relatives, and attending a *Tonight Show* taping has been a major priority of this trip.

There's a lipsticked blonde with electrocuted hair and her best friend—a homelier version of herself—who have just come from a taping of *The Dating Game*. They have been talking to boys from Minneapolis—now wearing California shorts and t-shirts—who want to be contestants on *The Dating Game*. They also want to be on camera tonight and fidget in their seats, hoping Johnny will come up into the audience.

In front of me, sit two typical American teen-agers, a sister and brother in punk hairdos with sweatshirts and jeans and Reebok sneakers. Part of a large family group, which seems to include uncles and aunts as well as parents, the kids are the only American-looking ones. As it turns out, none of this group is American. The entire gang is from the embassy of a Soviet Bloc nation. But the kids, raised amdist the malls and MTV stations of this country, are clearly "capitalist-roaders." (But the grown-ups will chortle delightedly, until they cough, at Johnny's jabs at politics, American and international.)

And then there are the rest of the fans: people in beehive hairdos; men in baseball caps; women in skin-tight trousers; oldsters in bowling jackets; yuppies dressed for success. It's an American audience. And they're all here. They're here to see *The Tonight Show*. As Ed, waving his papers, intones the words Here's

Johnny! the band pipes up into *Johnny's Theme* by Paul Anka, and the curtain opens.

When Johnny walks onto the stage, you see he is appealing; that's the first thing. The smile he has is a truly happy smile, and he plays not to the cameras but to us, the audience (though there is a bank of five monitors hanging from the rafters to help those of us in the audience to see the show).

People respond wildly; then Johnny goes into his monologue. We laugh and laugh, half from the jokes, half from the exuberance of being there. Then he recites the third joke. It dies. No one gets it. And Carson responds with a shocked look. It's not that the joke is bad. It's just that by the time of the third joke, the audience members aren't listening; they're looking, comparing the real Johnny with the TV image they know. He's warmer than he appears to be on the screen, smiling and nodding to fans and friends. By the time the audience realizes where it is, it also realizes it's forgotten to pay attention to Johnny's joke. He sighs in mock disbelief at the lack of laughter.

Then, with the years of experience begun one day in the thirties when a box of magic tricks from Chicago arrived at his Nebraska home, he makes the best of the lost joke and has the audience not only laughing but paying attention as well. With that "save," tonight's performance of *The Tonight Show* has truly begun.

The pros pay attention, too. McMahon, hearing the jokes for the first time, really does laugh. Severinsen and Tommy Newsom in the orchestra watch Johnny intently, as do the all the musicians. As often as they have worked this show, every night is a new night. Every night, even for the show's staffers, is a surprise. That's because the host has kept himself private, and secure. What we see and what McMahon, Severinsen, de Cordova, and the band sees, is the real item. Though he has a life away from us, he is the curious, bright, humorous, sometimes intense, sometimes vulnerable man we have come to know.

Twenty jokes later he finishes the monologue with his famous golf swing. While the monitors show the commercials, the lights on the set go down, and Carson moves to the desk. Once in his chair, he surveys his domain.

Severinsen nods a bow. McMahon moves closer and says something about the monologue. De Cordova waves some strange, but friendly signal. As the lights go back up to bright, Johnny beams at the studio audience. The cameras catch Johnny beaming.

Later it will be time for a presentation by the Mighty Carson Art Players; this episode will be a parody of home-shopping television shows. A spoof not only of greed, but of the vanity and egotism of television performers. The skit hits more often than it misses. In its wit, it is a monument to the late Fred Allen, the preeminent comedian and author whose skits and sketches taught Carson much of what he knows about satire and topical humor.

Today Johnny is the only performer in the country who parodies our national life and who makes fun of the headline news on a daily basis. There are other comedians, of course, who use politics as subject matter but they usually have some slick, super-hip angle to their jokes. Carson, like Allen, is the one whose wit is closest to the feelings and values of middle America.

The skit over, the show breaks for a commercial, and Johnny, *sans* shiny black wig, is back at his desk. He is ready for the guests. To aid him in his interviews is a set of note cards, which de Cordova placed on the desk moments before showtime. But Carson often ignores these. Unlike most talk-show hosts, he is so well read and well informed about the subject matter being discussed and about his guests, he doesn't need the notes, except occasionally for specific details, like the dates of a guest's upcoming appearances around the country, or the title and date of a movie or television show.

Even so, he doesn't have full control of the show—which sometimes means brilliant moments of spontaneous comedy and other times means not-so-entertaining slip-ups. Guest Bob Hope tonight has brought with him a *six-minute* promotional tape of his next NBC special. Carson watches it on the monitor, in seeming disbelief at its length. During the next commercial break, when Hope has finally departed, Carson berates de Cordova for letting the clip run so long. Then when singer Barbara Mandrel goes on for more than three minutes with a weird torch song about Santa, Carson turns away from her and talks quietly with McMahon.

But when a charmingly anachronistic ex-hippie comes on center stage to do some tricks with bubbles and a cigarette, Carson watches intently.

For the studio audience, which, unlike the home audience, does not have the opportunity during the show to get up and move about, the hour-long *Tonight Show*, entertaining as it is, seems longer. The amount of activity visible to the studio audience is so much greater—involving stage managers, stage hands, musicians, cameramen, microphone handlers, set decorators, directors, and nervous performers—that it's an exhausting, though enjoyable, hour.

Carson, however, is seemingly oblivious to all the activity. He is, of course, aware of it all, and knows to the second how much time he has for this or that segment. But he concentrates primarily on his audience and his guests. Most talk-show types are frantically watching the signals of the director, which can result in a distracted, rather anemic show, but Carson concentrates on the content. The technical aspects he mastered years ago. He works the technical stuff like a skilled long-distance trucker works his gears—easily, almost nonchalantly, but expertly.

The only sign of his nervousness is in his smoking. To his left—not visible to the TV audience—is an ashtray in which he manages to keep a cigarette burning at all times. During the commercial breaks, he puffs constantly.

Most of all, though, he enjoys the hour. He is the master of the talk show. He has survived challenges over the years from the likes of Dick Cavett, Merv Griffin, Joey Bishop, Alan Thicke, and most recently from a woman he made famous, Joan Rivers.

Joan, whose first important break in show business was a mid-sixties appearence on *The Tonight Show*, became Johnny's permanent guest host in 1983. In May 1986, however, she suddenly announced she was going to be hosting her own talk show on the new Fox Broadcasting Network. Johnny heard of this second hand—not from Joan herself. In light of all he had done for her, he felt that Rivers owed him at least the courtesy of a personal phone call. He said, "I am surprised, shocked, and disappointed. I am very upset at the manner with which this has been handled. It's very unusual. It's not the way I'm used to doing business. [Joan] used principles with which I am not familiar."

"That's shabby treatment," said Carson's amiable and expert public relations man, Jim Mahoney, of Rivers' behavior. "If she had gone to him and told him that she had a better offer, he would have congratulated her and wished her the best of luck."

Rivers had a $10 million contract from Fox, but less than a year after the show began, the Fox executives, troubled by her consistently low ratings and increasingly strident manner on the air, fired her. Radio commentator Paul Harvey described it as "the triumph of Nebraska over glitz." The latest talk-show wars, on the very eve of Johnny's twenty-fifth anniversary as the *The Tonight Show* host, ended with Johnny still victorious.

As the hour of the taping comes to a close, Johnny says good night, and the guests rise from the couch and chair. The band quiets down. Then the guests and Ed McMahon leave the set, and de Cordova leaves the stage. The cameras are off, and as Johnny walks off stage, he stops for a minute and looks towards the audience. He applauds them and waves. They stop gathering their things and applaud him. Then he goes off, alone, to his off-stage office. His night is over now. The day that began in Malibu with grump hour has finished with a shining hour.

Johnny still likes what he does. Though many—including Ed McMahon—thought Johnny would retire on the twenty-fifth anniversary of the show in October 1987, he has now signed a new contract with NBC to keep on going for another three years.

It's often a grind for him, and his show-business life has taken its toll on his personal life.

But as he has said, in America a man is his job. That's a national fact, and it's often a national tragedy. But it's a belief that produces greatness in some. Johnny has devoted himself to his job as a humorist—at enormous cost. But heroes aren't like the guy down the street; they do lead stranger, stronger, more expensive lives. The fortunate fact is that virtually everyone who has ever been associated with Johnny Carson—or related to him—wishes him well and feels kindly toward him.

The engima of Johnny's life is that he manages to speak so well, so humorously, and so clearly for middle America despite a lifestyle that's anything but middle class. How he does it, I still don't know, even after years studying his life. Ultimately,

CARSON

I don't really care how he does it. Like most Americans, instead, I just hope he keeps on doing it—speaking rambunctiously and humorously for us all. We wish him well, and hope that for many years there will be . . . more to come.

Index

A

Agnew, Spiro, 136, 175
Allen, Fred, 14, 60, 62, 67, 130, 139, 140, 230
Allen, Steve, 67, 87, 88-89, 90, 91, 104
Allen, Woody, 112, 128
Ames, Ed, 113
Amsterdam, Morey, 87, 88
Anderson, John, 170
Anderson, Norris, 57
Anka, Paul, 229
Arnoldi, Chuck, 19
Arquette, Cliff, 92
Austin, Howard, 201

B

Babbitt, Bruce, 138
Bankhead, Tallulah, 93
Beck, Marilyn, 172
Benny, Jack, 44, 62, 67, 69, 138-43, 146
Benny, Mary, 146
Bergen, Edgar, 76
Berle, Milton, 67
Biehl, Dr. J. Park, 214
Bishop, Joey, 102, 116, 120, 127, 128, 232
Brady, Ben, 70
Brady, Jim, 180
Brando, Marlon, 33
Brennan, Bill, 64-65
Brenner, David, 112
Brinkley, David, 109, 110
Brooks, Mel, 104
Brown, Edmund, 106-107
Brown, Jerry, 184-85
Bruno, Al, 73, 101, 122
Burns, George, 143
Bushkin, Mrs. Henry, 185-86
Bushkin, Henry, 163-66, 168, 185, 191, 205-206, 224

C

Carlin, George, 112
Carson, Alexandra (Alexis) (fourth wife), 13, 14, 19, 184, 187, 210, 217-25
Carson, Catherine (sister), 47, 177, 202
Carson, Chris (son), 65, 72, 73, 80, 82, 83-84, 177-78, 202-203, 204
Carson, Cory (son), 72, 73, 80, 82, 83-84, 177-78, 202-203, 204
Carson, Dick (brother), 24, 47, 57, 101, 129, 177, 202
Carson, Homer (Kit) (father), 46-47, 73, 177, 189, 202, 215
Carson, Joanna (third wife), 19, 39-40, 83, 100, 144, 145-48, 157, 159, 161, 173-79, 180-210, 218, 220
Carson, Joanne (second wife), 82, 99, 100-101, 118, 124, 131, 134, 145, 218
Carson, Jody (first wife), 57-58, 59, 64, 65-66, 68, 69, 72, 73, 80-83, 84, 85, 120-21, 184, 195, 197, 202-203, 225
Carson, Johnny:
childhood of, 46-52
in college, 56-59, 139
marriages, *see* Carson, Alexandra; Carson, Joanna; Carson, Joanne; Carson, Jody
movie experience, 80
in the navy, 54-55
night club act, 114, 215
in radio, 57, 59-60, 62
television experience, pre-*Tonight Show,* 58, 60-63, 65-72, 76-79, 84-86, 120
theater experience, 79-80

Tonight Show and, 20-38, 93, 97-98,
    100, 101-20, 122, 123, 125-127,
    129-31, 133-38, 143-44, 148-73,
    175-77, 179, 187, 192-93, 197,
    199, 207, 211-15, 225, 227-34
Carson, Ricky (son), 72, 73, 80, 82,
    83-84, 177-78, 202-203, 204
Carson, Ruth (mother), 47, 177, 202,
    204, 215-16
Carter, Jimmy, 137, 168, 170
Cass, Peggy, 92
Castro, Fidel, 93
Cavett, Dick, 27, 127-28, 129, 232
Chase, Chevy, 150-51, 159, 224
Christy, George, 182
Collins, Al, 91
Collins, Jackie, 194
Conried, Hans, 92
Cook, Ira, 67-68
Copeland, Joanne, *see* Carson,
    Joanne
Coren, Alan, 213-14
Cossette, Pierre, 40
Crawford, Joan, 104
Crowley, Arthur, 192
Cummings, Bob, 102

D
Davidson, John, 129
Davis, Bette, 20-21
Davis, Marvin, 224
Davis, Sammy, Jr., 122
Dean, Jimmy, 116, 117
de Cordova, Fred, 20, 24, 26,
    28, 32, 34, 35, 36-38, 119,
    129-30, 131, 138, 146, 149,
    159, 195, 197, 224, 227, 229, 230,
    231, 233
de Cordova, Janet, 182
Deeb, Gary, 155
de Moss, Mrs. Lyle, 63

de Moss, Lyle, 62, 63
de Vol, Frank, 68
Dickinson, Angie, 40
Dietrich, Marlene, 54
Dill, Guy, 19
Dole, Bob, 137
Donahue, Phil, 127, 129, 159
Douglas, Mike, 112, 127, 129
DuBrow, Rick, 136
Dukakis, Michael, 220, 221

F
Fay, Frank, 141
Fedderson, Don, 76
Fein, Irving, 138, 139
Fischoff, Richard, 187, 190
Fontaine, Frank, 140
Forrestal, James, 55
Fountain, Peter, 21
Francis, Arlene, 79, 102
Francis, Connie, 80
Franer, John, 49
Froelich, Harold V., 135
Frost, David, 127, 129
Funt, Allen, 75

G
Gardella, Kay, 160-61
Garland, Judy, 93
Genevieve, 92
Gleason, Jackie, 141
Gobel, George, 143, 144
Gold, Betty, 19
Goodman, Ellen, 194
Goosen, Donna, 49-50
Gordon, Fay, 50-51, 52, 81
Gorme, Eydie, 90
Gould, Jack, 71
Graham, Billy, 129
Graham, Robert, 19
Graham, Virginia, 127, 129

Grant, Arnold, 117
Graziano, Rocky, 99
Greco, Buddy, 127
Greene, Gael, 97-98
Griffin, Merv, 101, 127, 128-29, 232

H
Hackett, Buddy, 92
Hamilton, George, 80
Hardy, Oliver, 141
Harrington, Pat, Jr., 92
Hartley, Mariette, 125, 148
Harvey, Paul, 233
Hayakawa, S.I., 137
Havard, James, 19
Hayes, Peter Lind, 102
Healy, Mary, 102
Helmsley, Sherman, 28
Henderson, Skitch, 90
Heston, Charlton, 21, 128
Hockney, David, 19
Holland, Joanna, *see* Carson,
    Joanna
Holland, Tim, 145
Holland, Tim, Jr., 145, 146
Hope, Bob, 136, 139, 140, 143, 160,
    231
Hopper, Hedda, 149
Hudson, Rock, 29-30
Hughes, Howard, 100
Humphrey, Hubert, 133
Huntley, Chet, 109, 110
Hurlbert, Jack, 48-49, 56

I
Isaacs, Charlie, 70-71

J
James, Dennis, 124
Jardin, Eugene, 19
Johns, Emily, 185, 186

K
Kane, Paul, 19
Kennedy, Edward, 105
Kennedy family, 93
Kerlin, Doris, 49, 56
Kilgallen, Dorothy, 93
King, Alexander, 92
Knotts, Don, 90
Kovacs, Ernie, 91

I
Lampert, Stuart, 19
Lawrence, Steve, 21, 90, 102
Lazar, Irving "Swifty," 39, 41
Leary, Timothy, 129
Lee, Robert E., 112
Lemmon, Jack, 128
Lennon, John, 171
Leonard, Jack E., 88, 102
LeRoy, Mervyn, 200
Lescoulie, Jack, 91
Lester, Jerry, 87, 88
Letterman, David, 171
Lewis, Jerry, 102
Liederman, David, 220-21
Linkletter, Art, 102
Lloyd, David, 27

M
McCormick, Pat, 31
McEnroe, John, 19
McEnroe, Tatum, 19
McMahon, Ed, 15, 24, 26, 31,
    33-34, 35, 38, 84, 111, 116, 117,
    119, 122, 141, 211, 227-29, 230,
    231, 233
McMahon, John, 225
Mahoney, Jim, 232
Man, Alberto, 19
Mandrel, Barbara, 231
Mansfield, Irving, 98-99

Mantle, Mickey, 31
March, Hal, 102, 121
Maris, Roger, 31
Martin, Dean, 143
Martin, Steve, 40, 41, 159, 224
Marx, Groucho, 14, 77, 101, 102
Mass (also "Maas"), Alexandra, *see*
   Carson, Alexandra
Mauk, Gene, 50
Maxwell, Elsa, 92
Milland, Ray, 112
Mitchell, Dolores, 221
Mitchell, Pat, 220
Mizumo, Peter Shire, 19
Mulholland, Kevin, 26
Murray, Arthur, 72
Murray, Jan, 102, 121
Murray, Kathryn, 72

N
Narz, Jack, 120-24
Newhart, Bob, 20, 116, 195
Newsom, Tommy, 141, 229
Newton, Wayne, 166
Niles, Ed, 18, 19
Nimo, Bill, 122
Nixon, Richard, 93, 105, 106-107,
   129, 135-36
Nye, Louis, 90

O
O'Connor, Donald, 102

P
Paar, Jack, 91-95, 97, 98, 101, 102,
   103, 115, 120, 127, 128
Parnis, Molly, 146, 147, 184
Petrashek, Richard "Pete," 61-63
Pierce, Fred, 161
Pleshette, Suzanne, 125, 149
Poston, Tom, 90

Prentiss, Paula, 80
Provenza, Paul, 21
Pryor, Richard, 112
Pudney, Gary, 161

Q
Quinn, Bobby, 37

R
Randall, Tony, 148
Rayburn, Gene, 89, 90
Reagan, Ronald, 127, 131, 137,
   170-171
Reckert, Bob, 49
Reed, Marjorie, 183-84
Rickles, Don, 100, 123
Rivers, Joan, 21, 26, 30, 113, 190,
   196, 232
Rosenfield, Paul, 20, 21
Rule, Elton, 161

S
Sahl, Mort, 102
Sajak, Pat, 24, 65
Sales, Soupy, 102
Sanford, Larry, 50, 51-52
Sargent, Herb, 102
Sarnoff, Jan, 184, 196
Schmidt, Dorn, 18
Schweitzer, Albert, 93
Selleck, Tom, 222
Severinsen, Doc, 21, 24, 34, 35, 37,
   38, 141, 227, 229, 230
Shawn, Dick, 150, 151
Shields, Tom, 122
Shriner, Herb, 139
Silverman, Fred, 60, 155, 156, 157,
   159, 160, 169, 170, 211-12
Sinatra, Frank, 143, 183
Skelton, Red, 62, 67, 68-69
Smilgis, Martha, 41

Smith, Liz, 166, 188, 189
Snyder, Tom, 148, 159, 160
Sozting, Catherine (née Carson), 47, 177
Sozting, Jeff, 177
Spelling, Aaron, 158
Spiller, Raymond, 26
Stark, Art, 76, 77, 78, 79, 101, 103, 116, 118-19
Steeples, Joe, 213
Stewart, Jimmy, 224
Sullivan, Ed, 93
Susann, Jacqueline, 98-99
"Suzy" (columnist), 188-89

T
Taylor, Elizabeth, 129
Tebet, Dave, 156, 171
Tellez, Rudy, 119
Tennis, Craig, 126
Thicke, Alan, 212, 232
Thomopolous, Tony, 161
Tinker, Grant, 212
Tiny Tim and Miss Vicki, 31, 126-27, 131, 133
Tomar, Steven, 19
Twain, Mark, 14
Tynan, Kenneth, 53

U
Ulrich, Peter, 185, 186

V
Vallee, Rudy, 104
Van Dyke, Dick, 76
Van Horne, Harriet, 79-80
Vasa, 19
Vidal, Gore, 201
Vollbracht, Michael, 184, 208-09

W
Wadowitz, Father, 122
Wallace, Mike, 25, 155, 168
Wayne, Carol, 131
Weaver, Sylvester "Pat," 89, 90
Weinberger, Ed, 27-28
Welles, Orson, 54, 128
Werblin, Sonny, 164
Wetzel, Dean, 49
White, Betty, 92
White, Timothy, 25
White, Vanna, 24
Wilder, Billy, 20
Williams, Andy, 90
Williams, Bob, 106-107
Wilson, Drue, 26
Wolcott, Jody, see Carson, Jody
Wood, Shirley, 31
Woodbury, Woody, 79
Woods, Rosemary, 135

Y
Youngman, Henny, 129

239